JORDEN BEACON

Wholesaling Real Estate Business

A Beginner's Guide to Profitable Deals

Copyright © 2024 by Jorden Beacon

All rights reserved. No part of this publication may be reproduced, stored or transmitted in any form or by any means, electronic, mechanical, photocopying, recording, scanning, or otherwise without written permission from the publisher. It is illegal to copy this book, post it to a website, or distribute it by any other means without permission.

First edition

Contents

I   Getting Started with Real Estate Wholesaling

1 Understanding the Basics of Wholesaling	3
What is wholesale trade?	3
Types of Wholesale Trade	5
Differences between Wholesale and Retail	6
Advantages of Wholesale Business	7
Common wholesaler mistakes	7
The main problems of wholesale sales	8
Effective methods to increase wholesale sales	11
How to open and organize the wholesale trade process	14
Laws and taxation of wholesale trade	15
2 Developing a Strategic Mindset for Success	16
Types of pricing strategies in retail sales	17
Price Based on Competition	18
Fixed markup to product costs	19
Discount prices	19
Selling below cost	20
Discount	20
Penetration price	21
'Cream harvesting' strategy	22
Value-based strategy	22
Target price	23
Price psychology, or the ending "99"	23

Bundle prices	24
Price discrimination	25
Dynamic price management	25
Geographical price differentiation	26
Prestige pricing strategy	26
base price	27
Development of a pricing strategy	27
There are a few things you need to keep in mind when implementing a new pricing strategy	30
Combining strategies	32
3 Building a Strong Foundation for Your Business	34
Advantages of wholesale business	35
How to understand what to trade in the wholesale business	35
Participants and logic of wholesale trade	36
What agreement to conclude with a supplier in the field of wholesale trade	38
Is it possible to start a wholesale business from scratch without large investments?	38
How to open a wholesale business: instructions	39
How to increase sales in a wholesale business	40
How to find regular customers in a wholesale business	41
4 Leveraging Technology and Automation	43
Advantages of wholesale trade automation systems	44
Implementation of CRM. From lead registration to deal closure	46
What is needed to implement a CRM system?	52

II Mastering Wholesaling Techniques

5 Finding Lucrative Real Estate Deals	57
Real Estate Investment Goals	57

Pros and cons of investing in real estate	58
What kind of real estate can you invest in?	59
How risky is it to invest in real estate?	60
Ways to invest in real estate	61
Procedure for investing in real estate	64
How to make more money in real estate	64
6 10 Ways to Motivate Employees	66
1. Renaming the position	66
2. Team spirit	67
3. Comfort	68
4. Training	70
5. Career growth	70
6. Non-standard nominations	71
7. Gamification	72
8. Balance	72
9. Gratitude	73
10. Humanity	74
7 Promotion Of Wholesale Sales	76
Specifics of Wholesale Sales	76
Wholesale Sales Indicators	78
How can a wholesale company attract large customers	79
When is it necessary to take measures to promote wholesale sales?	79
Standard methods of promoting wholesale sale	80
Wholesale Marketing	82
Working with the client-based	84
What should a website be like to promote wholesale trade?	86
How to promote a wholesale website	88
8 Working with Objections in Sales- How to do it...	91
Common sales objections and how to deal with them	92

Best Practices for Handling Sales Objections — 95

III Scaling Your Wholesaling Business

9 Scale up and maximize profits: Using CRM to Grow your... — 101
What are CRM systems? — 102
Benefits of using CRM systems to scale your business — 103
Steps to successfully scaling your business — 105
10 How do we build the perfect team to make cooperation... — 108
What is a team? — 108
What are the advantages of building a team that achieves set goals? — 109
How to build an effective team? — 109
11 How to build an effective and efficient team of employees? — 112
4 essential tools that will help a manager create an effective and efficient team — 112
How else can a manager improve team effectiveness? — 115
12 How to Grow Your Business Through Marketing — 117
Set your business growth goals — 118
Find out about your target audience — 119
Explore the short-term field of marketing — 119
Double down on what works — 119
Create an SEO Friendly Website — 120
Focus on marketing strategies you have time for — 121
Encourage satisfied customers to leave reviews — 122
Track progress and make changes — 123
13 Optimizing Your Business for Long-Term Success — 124
Continuous Learning and Skill Development — 124
Change management — 130

IV Advanced Strategies and Tips for Wholesaling Success

14 How to attract financing for a business at different stages	137
Why investment is needed	137
Stages of company development	138
Types of Business Finance	139
How to choose the type of financing	139
Principles of searching for investors	140
Sources of funding for startups	140
Sources of financing at the stages of business expansion and growth	142
Business valuation methods	144
15 Management of Legal Risks and Legal Issues	145
Customized solutions and actionable analytics	146
A proven four-step approach	146
16 Negotiation strategies	148
Global Negotiation Conditions	149
Features of negotiations involving more than two opponents	152
Negotiation Strategies	153
17 Developing Strategic Thinking	160
How does strategy differ from tactics?	160
Principles of Strategic Thinking	161
Skills that help develop strategic thinking	164
How to develop strategic thinking	165

I

Getting Started with Real Estate Wholesaling

1

Understanding the Basics of Wholesaling

Wholesale trade operates effectively in the online and offline environment. The mechanism for the functioning of this tactic for selling goods is built on the sale of large quantities of products, most often intended for subsequent resale.

Wholesale buyers do not interact with end consumers but act as a link in market turnover. Market participants act as intermediaries, work with large volumes of products, and are engaged in the purchase, warehousing, and marketing of goods purchased from manufacturers.

What is wholesale trade?

Retail sales of goods involve the delivery of a product or service directly to the consumer. Wholesale trade "works" on a different principle. First, the goods are supplied to companies, marked up, and then sold to ordinary customers.

In simple words, a wholesaler is a trading organization that cooperates with product manufacturers and customers to whom these products are sold. The difference between a wholesaler and a distributor is that a wholesaler can simultaneously interact with different manufacturing companies, even within "non-overlapping" product groups. A distributor, as a rule, sells goods purchased from one manufacturer or wholesaler to retail chains. Cooperation with wholesalers is beneficial for many market participants:

1. The product manufacturer gets the opportunity to quickly sell the product in large quantities at a set price below the retail price. Benefits of the enterprise: you can sell large volumes of goods and not waste time searching for distribution channels.
2. Distributors only need to concentrate on one serious wholesaler client to purchase products at an attractive price. Advantages for the distributor: meeting deadlines for delivery of goods to "their" retail stores.
3. Retail chains cooperate either directly with wholesalers or work through distributors. In both options, stores do not have to waste time purchasing products from many places. It is enough to establish partnerships with counterparties.

Retail stores, even with extensive networks, rarely work directly with manufacturers, since this is inconvenient for the manufacturers themselves. Traders will not be able to buy goods in large quantities and accurately indicate the range and volumes in advance due to the specifics of supply and demand. Therefore, it is more profitable for both parties to work through intermediaries represented by wholesalers.

Important! For retail, wholesale sales are profitable. They provide access to a wide range of manufacturers' products, provided by wholesalers at an attractive price. Retailers still have the opportunity to make such a markup on goods so that the final cost is affordable to end consumers, but at the same time, the store does not work to its detriment.

Types of Wholesale Trade

The average wholesaler sells 5,000 items of goods. The formula for the success of a trading company: assortment - volumes - delivery to location - turnover of goods - planning - loans and deferred payments. Each element of the chain must work efficiently. Expanding the assortment does not always help increase sales, and hiring a good salesperson does not necessarily lead to an increase in company profits.

Wholesale trade can take two main forms. Transit sales are the sale of goods without storage in the wholesaler's warehouse. For the company, this option is simpler and cheaper. Warehouse turnover involves the sale of products from the warehouses of a wholesaler. In addition, there are different types of wholesale trade:

1. Through a wholesale purchasing network. The company sells goods subject to storage through food markets, auctions, fairs, and exchanges.
2. Trade through direct production connections is most typical for the ferrous metals market.
3. Trade in raw materials and supplies.

The last type of wholesale sales is further classified into several categories:

1. with centralized delivery;
2. upon receipt of goods from the supplier;
3. with payment in cash before acceptance and transportation;

4. wholesale trade from racks.

Wholesalers work in the market, purchasing products of different assortments. Therefore, experts distinguish two more types of wholesale trade - the sale of a wide range of goods and specialized wholesale trade. In the first case, the wholesaler collects a wide range of goods from different groups. In specialized trade, an in-depth assortment of products from one product group is sold.

Differences between Wholesale and Retail

We've figured out what is considered wholesale trade and belongs to the relevant industry - it's time to move into the topic a little deeper. In the modern world, any product, before reaching the final consumer, passes through many intermediary organizations. The manufacturer ships the goods to a regional wholesaler, who divides the batch into parts and sends them to smaller traders, who, in turn, redirect the rest to stores.

The difference between wholesale and retail is colossal. In the first case, we are talking about the interaction of entrepreneurs with each other, and in the second, about the shipment of inventory items in favor of the end consumer. Five key factors make it possible to separate one area from another:

1. **Target audience** - Marketing campaigns and positioning for large customers do not work;
2. **Volumes** - Sale of products in large bundles, with transportation by road trains, railway cars, and sea tankers;
3. **Markup** - On average 3-5%, making a profit not through added value, but through mass sales;

4. **Transaction cycles**—Wholesale buyers spend enormous amounts of time vetting suppliers, analyzing the market, and calculating economics;
5. **Working with the client base** - Focusing on b2b, not b2c, collecting detailed information about possible partners.

Wholesalers who want to achieve commercial success have to create special promotion strategies.

Advantages of Wholesale Business

For their complex and quite risky business activities, companies interacting with large parties receive the following bonuses:

1. **Big deals** - Impressive turnover figures, which are almost impossible to achieve in retail;
2. **Extensive geography** - Presence in many national markets simultaneously;
3. **Optimization of marketing costs** - Other businessmen will learn about a good counterparty without advertising.

However, each advantage has its nuances - an extended sales cycle, the need to draw up complex accompanying documentation for border control, and the lack of periodically profitable contact with direct consumers due to insufficiently active promotion.

Common wholesaler mistakes

Carrying out activities in the field of wholesale trade online or through physical sales is not immune to errors. This is due to shortcomings in building, organizing, and running a business. Errors lead to a shortage of funds, violation of delivery deadlines, and termination of contracts by counterparties. The most common "mistakes" at work:

- the company does not have a clear sales planning system;
- starting investments are initially distributed incorrectly;
- there is no interaction between structural units;
- the company is in debt and cannot fulfill its obligations;
- there is no understanding of the needs of the target audience.

A thorough market analysis before launching a business, drawing up a competent strategic plan and confident management of the company help prevent possible risks for a business. Investments should first be directed to the development of product supply channels, and then solve less priority problems.

On a note! Coordination of business processes in a single information field, the presence of a functional financial department to control the budget and the adoption of legal measures to protect the interests of the company help to avoid mistakes in wholesale sales.

The main problems of wholesale sales

Despite all the advantages, wholesale trade is not without its disadvantages. Companies operating in this area face serious difficulties, which are often critical for wholesalers. It is worth taking a closer look at the most serious problems of wholesale sales.

Leverage not available

If the wholesaler has not paid for the previous shipment of goods, creditor confidence rapidly declines. This is manifested in the limitation of the volume of financial resources. There is a shortage of funds to purchase a new batch of goods. The problem can be caused by the length of time it takes to sell the previous batch due to a drop in demand for the product, which leads to the illiquidity of the product. If the wholesaler was unable to quickly sell the batch due to too large a purchase, surplus products form in the warehouse.

Retailers are failing

The wholesaler cooperates with retail companies. There is always a high risk that the organization will change its work profile or completely cease its activities. As a result, no one will buy a batch of goods from the wholesaler. And the products may have already been paid for by the manufacturing company. The store owner does not care much that wholesale sales are planned for his company if problems arise with the business. As a result, the wholesaler will have to re-plan his work, especially when collaborating with a store on deferred payment.

Customer fickleness can manifest itself in other ways. For example, a retail company is scaling its operations and needs to increase its supply volumes. A wholesale company plans purchases at least six months in advance. It is not always possible to simply purchase additional goods from the manufacturer because the company needs time to manufacture the product. The wholesaler can either reduce supplies of similar goods to other stores, or insist on additional purchases from the manufacturer.

Attention! Situations, when retailers refuse remaining products due to lack of money and offer the wholesaler to pick up the goods seriously, spoil planning for wholesale sales. As a result, the trading company has to replan its financial and organizational activities.

Violation of delivery deadlines from the manufacturer

The wholesaler has contracts with both sides of the commodity relationship - with the manufacturer and with the retail company. For some reason, the manufacturer may not be able to release the product within the specified time frame. Or he has problems at customs, along the way of cargo delivery, defective goods, etc. As a result, the wholesale company has nothing to supply to the retail network, which results in penalties and termination of the contract. The wholesaler's reputation suffers, and interactions with counterparties are disrupted.

Influence of the human factor

Incorrect forecasting of demand and errors in planning are the consequences of the influence of the human factor on the work. The head of the wholesale company himself, his managers, and lower-level employees can make a mistake. Wholesale companies face common problems:

- Dismissal of a valuable employee and departure along with the customer base;
- Refusal of clients to cooperate due to incorrect work;
- Incorrect actions of supply specialists and logisticians.

The human factor can provoke serious consequences for a wholesale company: the formation of illiquid balances, blocking of working capital, overcrowding of warehouse space, cash gaps, supply interruptions, and other negative aspects.

Need for structural changes

A wholesale company is more interested in meeting the current demand of existing retail customers than in finding new customers. One wholesaler cooperates with many manufacturers and retail stores and handles large quantities of goods presented in a wide range.

For the successful functioning of the company, mid-level specialists, warehouses, and transport are needed. For this chain to work smoothly, it is required:

- Enter measurements into the staffing table;
- Expand sales departments and the number of suppliers;
- Automate business processes;
- Plan work in the long term;
- Forecast purchase and sales volumes.

All this is influenced by time, the human factor, the availability of finished products from the manufacturer, the solvency of retailers, etc. Therefore, for wholesalers, a clear structure for the purchase, storage, and delivery of goods is of primary importance.

Effective methods to increase wholesale sales

To sell products faster, a wholesaler would benefit from an online presence. Having your website helps to attract the target audience, establish prompt customer service, and eliminate errors in documentation. There are effective ways to increase sales.

Transparent pricing

Wholesalers' prices depend on transportation costs and the pricing policies of manufacturing companies. It is important to understand that lower prices do not always stimulate sales growth. This is because such promotions cause distrust among customers. Price tags for goods must be set so that potential customers do not consider them too high or low, and the wholesaler himself can make a profit from sales.

The expansion of the customer base

We are talking about increasing the sales of online wholesale stores by attracting more customers. To do this, you can use different programs, for example, auto-dialing, advertising to the target audience, negotiations, discounts on complex purchases, promotional offers for regular customers, etc.

Automation of business processes

To reduce the influence of the human factor and optimize the working time of employees, assistant programs are used. They simplify the data processing process and provide effective integration with the store. Using the programs is convenient for forming a customer base, maintaining statistics, and managing finances.

Customer failure analysis

Wholesalers often face a situation where the customer refuses to supply. The reasons for this may be different: there are no funds to pay, the supplier ordered the wrong product, the client did not like the service, and prices are inflated. Failures of even small customer firms need to be analyzed to eliminate the problem.

Improving the product range

Trading companies deal with a long list of products. But there is always the opportunity to expand the range and add related products to the list. First, you need to analyze the sales dynamics and highlight the most popular and in-demand products. But you shouldn't get too carried away with expanding the range - this increases costs.

Efficient logistics department

The employees of this division will have to provide the company with a continuous cycle of wholesale sales. The competent work of logisticians helps to establish interaction with counterparties and prevent delays in deliveries. Having an in-house logistics department gives a wholesaler a strong competitive advantage.

Wholesale sales are an important link in the trade chain. Manufacturers have the opportunity to quickly sell large quantities of products. Retail chain stores have access to a wide range of products. And all this happens through the intermediary of wholesale trading companies.

How to open and organize the wholesale trade process

This is where the sales funnel comes into play - it is what allows you to put retail procedures on stream, dividing them into key stages. You can understand how effectively a system created by your department or third-party experts functions through a simple analysis. The numbers of consumers are entered in a separate chart:

1. phoned trade managers;
2. received a commercial offer;
3. who have agreed on a direct business meeting;
4. who spoke with a consultant live;
5. who have entered into the necessary agreement;
6. those who picked up the consignment of goods from the first shipment;
7. returned for further cooperation.

Visualization of the presented table (using the same business programs) will be a reflection of the current funnel. If certain numbers drop, that's what you should focus on when developing a promotion strategy. For example, customers may be cut off at the stage of concluding agreements. Then the problem will be either the incompetence of the salesperson or a frankly weak USP.

In this chapter, we explained what underlies wholesale sales, what rules and conditions must be followed when trading wholesale, what is the essence of the methods of conducting this type of business, and what operating principle must be followed in the face of changing market requirements. Let us summarize: to stimulate the economic development of a company, it is necessary to introduce innovative technologies into work, give preference to digitalization, and automate routine.

Laws and taxation of wholesale trade

Many people call wholesale the sale of goods in large quantities, retail – individual sales. This statement is only partly true. Law No. 381-FZ dated December 28, 2009, gives a different definition to the concepts of retail and wholesale trade. In simple words, the meaning of legislative terms can be interpreted as follows:

- when goods are purchased for business purposes, this is wholesale trade;
- if products are purchased for personal home use, this is retail trade.

Of course, the store seller has no idea what the buyer does with the product after purchase - uses it himself or resells it to another consumer. You can distinguish wholesale from retail by the presence of contracts. Wholesale sales are formalized between the seller (wholesaler) and the buyer (business entity) by a purchase and sale agreement or a supply agreement. Trade relations between the owner of a retail store and an individual buyer are formalized by a simple cash receipt.

Important! If an entrepreneur plans to open a trading company for wholesale sales, you need to choose the legal form of the enterprise (IP or LLC) and the taxation system. You can pay taxes using a simplified scheme or on a general basis - the tax rate varies.

2

Developing a Strategic Mindset for Success

In today's competitive retail market, it is more important than ever to have a clear and well-defined pricing strategy. Pricing strategy is an element of the management process, a plan according to which a company prices its products and services. However, it is more complex than it may seem. There are many factors to consider, such as:

1. Cost of goods
2. Desired margin
3. Profit
4. Demand
5. Prices
6. Supply of competitive products

Sellers use various ways to increase sales and attract new customers. Pricing based on specific strategies helps you achieve this goal.

Some of the most commonly used tactics include:

1. Manufacturer's suggested retail price
2. Comparative (competitive) price
3. Adding a fixed percentage markup to the product cost
4. Psychological pricing tactics
5. Penetration price
6. Discount price
7. Base price
8. Selling below cost

In this chapter, we'll take a closer look at pricing strategies and provide some tips for developing and implementing effective retail pricing tactics to gain a competitive advantage and maintain your company's profitability.

Types of pricing strategies in retail sales

Retailers use different pricing strategies to price their products and services. Choosing the best pricing model will depend on many individual factors, so you should carefully determine the characteristics of your company, your needs, and your expectations.

The huge variety of pricing strategies include:

MSRP

MSRP, or Manufacturer's Suggested Retail Price, is a classic example of pricing policy. What is it? This is simply using the price that the manufacturer recommends for its products at retail. As a rule, MSRP is usually higher than the wholesale price that a retailer pays when purchasing a product, as it assumes a markup by the retailer.

MSRP is the starting point for most retailers when pricing their products. It takes into account production costs, expected margins, and market competition.

Advantages :

- Easy to calculate
- It gives the client a point of reference

Defects :

- It may turn out to be higher than customers are willing to pay
- Competitors may price cheaper

Price Based on Competition

The competitive price is based on reference to the current prices of competitive products. Such a strategy may involve setting the same prices as the competition or setting the level slightly below the competition's prices. This method is quite commonly used by companies selling in highly competitive markets.

Advantages :

- It helps to capture a certain part of the market
- It can help increase margins

Defects :

- May cause price wars
- Difficult to maintain.

Fixed markup to product costs

Fixed markup pricing refers to a situation in which the seller uses a constant markup added to the cost of the product to set prices. Typically, the markup is defined as a percentage of costs, but it can also be defined as an amount. This strategy allows for a simple calculation method but does not take into account competitors' activities or customer expectations.

Advantages:

- Ease of calculations
- It allows you to maintain the assumed margin level

Defects:

- Prices may be too high in reality, but also too low in terms of the market
- It may not meet customer requirements

Discount prices

Discount pricing strategies involve temporary reductions in the retail price of a product or service. It's just that a cheap product is always easier to sell than an expensive one. The lure of low prices is usually intended to increase sales or clear inventory. Discounts can take many forms, such as a percentage off, buy one product, get one free, or free shipping.

Advantages:

- They help in increasing sales
- They can help clean warehouses

Defects :

- They can lead to lower profits
- They can accustom customers to only buying products on sale

Selling below cost

Products priced this way are often sold at a loss to attract customers to the store or website. This is associated with the expectation that customers interested in these products will buy other, more profitable for the seller. This pricing strategy is usually used by companies that have a large selection of products.

Advantages :

- Helps attract customers
- This may lead to sales of other products

Defects :

- It may generate losses
- In the long run, it may be unprofitable

Discount

The strategy of preventive pricing assumes setting prices at a level that discourages competitors from entering the market, while at the same time allowing them to cover production costs and generate a profit.

Such tactics are usually used by companies with a very large share, or simply monopolists in a given industry.

Advantages :

- It allows you to maintain market share
- It can ensure profitability

Defects :

- The prices may turn out to be too high
- It may discourage customers from making a purchase

Penetration price

A penetration strategy involves setting a lower price for a product or service to gain market share. This pricing strategy is usually used when a new company wants to enter the market or introduces a new product or service.

Advantages :

- It allows you to gain market share
- It allows you to increase sales

Defects :

- May reduce profits
- In the long run, it may be unprofitable

'Cream harvesting' strategy

This strategy involves charging a high price for a product or service to maximize profits. This pricing strategy is usually used by companies when they introduce a new product to the market. After an initial period, you can start lowering prices to attract more price-sensitive customers.

Advantages :

- It allows you to maximize profit
- Helps recover production costs

Defects :

- May reduce sales
- It may discourage customers from making purchases

Value-based strategy

A value-based pricing strategy is when a company determines its retail price based on the customer's perceived value of the product or service. This pricing strategy takes into account the customer's needs and expectations, as well as the competition.

Advantages :

- It helps ensure that customers will be willing to pay
- It allows you to distinguish a product or service from the competition

Defects:

- It may be difficult to calculate
- The result may be prices that are too low or too high

Target price

Setting a target price involves determining the price of a product or service based on market analysis and the expected margin. Then the cost of the product is determined. This pricing strategy takes into account competition, customer demand, and expected margin.

Advantages:

- It helps ensure the expected margin or profit
- It allows you to control costs

Defects:

- The result may be too low or too high prices
- It may not take into account the customer's requirements

Price psychology, or the ending "99"

Psychological pricing is a pricing tactic that uses customers' psychological characteristics to set prices. It can take various forms, such as "just below" prices, multiple items, crossed-out prices, etc. A perfect example is a price change from "PLN 10" to "9.99". There is no difference for the store, but the customer responds psychologically much better to it. This price psychology trick is widely used, especially in hypermarkets, because it works perfectly. Prices ending in 9 groszy, instead of the full amount, make the products more attractive to the human mind.

Advantages :

- Enables you to increase sales
- It can help you increase your margin

Defects :

- The result may be too low or too high prices
- It may not work in the long term

Bundle prices

Bundling pricing means selling two or more products or services as a set at a discounted price. This pricing strategy is typically used to increase sales, clear inventory, or attract customers.

Advantages :

- It allows you to increase sales
- It allows you to clean warehouses
- It can attract customers

Defects :

- May reduce profit

Price discrimination

Price discrimination involves different prices of the same product or service for different customers, depending on how much they are willing to pay. For this pricing strategy to be successful, the company must have a dominant market share, a unique product, exclusive sales, etc.

Advantages :

- It allows you to maximize profit
- Helps increase sales

Defects :

- The result may be too low or too high prices
- It may not work in the long term
- It can damage your brand's reputation

Dynamic price management

Dynamic pricing is a strategy involving dynamic price changes product or services based on real-time demand. This pricing strategy is typically used by companies selling products or services with limited availability, such as concert tickets or hotel rooms.

Advantages :

- Ensures prices are adequate for current demand
- It can help you maximize your profit

Defects :

- May reduce sales
- It may discourage customers from making a purchase

Geographical price differentiation

Geographic pricing is a practice in which companies set prices based on the location of customers. This pricing strategy is typically used by companies with a large geographic reach, such as online stores.

Advantages :

- It helps to match prices to demand
- It allows you to increase your margin

Defects :

- The result may be too low or too high prices
- It may not work in the long term

Prestige pricing strategy

A prestige pricing strategy usually means a high price for a product or service. This pricing strategy is typically used for luxury goods or products with high perceived value, usually available in limited quantities.

Advantages :

- It allows you to maximize profits

- Helps increase margins
- It allows you to build a premium brand reputation

Defects:

- This may result in reduced sales
- It may discourage customers from making a purchase

base price

Base pricing involves setting the retail price at twice the wholesale price. So, if the wholesale price of a product is PLN 10, the retail price will be PLN 20. This pricing strategy is usually used by companies that have a large market share or monopolies.

Advantages:

1. It can help protect market share
2. Helps ensure profitability

Defects:

- The result may be too high prices

Development of a pricing strategy

There is no one universal pricing strategy for everyone. Choosing the best one will depend on many individual factors, including the type of products or services sold, reasonable margins, demand, and competition in the market.

Now that we've looked at some of the most commonly used pricing strategies, it's time to start developing a pricing strategy.

Here are some tips to help you get started:

Define your business goals

The first step in developing a pricing strategy is to define your business goals. What do you want to achieve with your pricing strategy? Do you want to increase sales, improve margins, or acquire new customers?

Your business goals should be specific, measurable, achievable, relevant, and time-bound.

Recognize the costs

To develop an effective retail pricing strategy, you need to start by analyzing your costs. It includes not only the costs of producing the goods or services sold but also the costs of running a business, such as rent, labor, utilities, payroll, and marketing. Knowing your costs will help you set a price that covers them while still leaving room for profit.

Once you have a good understanding of your costs, you can begin to develop a pricing strategy that meets the expected margin.

Define the required profit

After considering all the above factors, you need to determine your desired profitability. It means the amount you want to earn on each sale.

To calculate this amount, you need to know what your gross margin is. Gross margin is a measure expressed as a percentage of the difference between the selling price and the costs associated with producing the product and the selling price.

Define your target market and acquire new customers

The next step is to analyze the target market. Who is your ideal client? What are his needs and desires? How much is he willing to pay for your product or service?

The answers to these questions will help you optimally price your products and services.

Get to know the customer's requirements

Then you need to identify customer needs. This includes determining how much customers are willing to pay for your products or services, as well as what motivates them to make a purchase.

Once you have accurate information about what demand is, you can start developing tactics that will appeal to your customers.

Research the competition

Finally, take a closer look at your competition. Monitor the prices your competitors charge for their products or services, but also their overall pricing strategy.

What are their strengths and weaknesses? How do their prices compare to your costs? The answers to these questions will help you better position your products and services in the market. Remember that this is not about mindless imitation.

If you've already researched the competition, you can create competitive pricing strategies that will give you an advantage.

Implementing pricing strategies

Finally, when you have analyzed everything and created the optimal pricing strategy for your products and services, you need to make sure that it is implemented effectively, but also that it is effective.

There are a few things you need to keep in mind when implementing a new pricing strategy

1. Set your prices to meet your goals

Above all, make sure your pricing aligns with your business goals, whether that's increasing sales, improving margins, or attracting new customers. Make sure your pricing is consistent with these goals.

2. Don't be afraid to test different pricing tactics

Secondly, don't be afraid to test prices. It's important to find the right price for your products and services, but it can be a difficult task. A good way to find the right price is to test different methods and see how customers respond.

This can be done by offering discounts, organizing promotions or simply changing the price of a product or service for a specific period.

You can useA/B testing to check different prices and see which one generates the most sales. This will help you refine your pricing strategy and ensure its effectiveness.

3. Train employees

Then you need to train your employees on your new pricing strategy. They will be the ones who implement it daily. They need to know how to properly price products and services and present them appropriately to customers.

Providing employees needed tools and training will allow them to effectively implement the new pricing strategy and achieve the desired results.

4. Inform your customers about changes

When you're ready to implement your new pricing strategy, communicate the changes to your customers. This will help them understand the reasons for the changes and how they will affect them.

You can communicate changes to your customers through various channels such as your website, email, social media, or even directly in-store.

5. Use technology

In today's digital world, some many online programs and tools can help you update prices automatically based on market changes. This will help you stay competitive and avoid having to manually update prices, which is time-consuming and error-producing.

Some many different applications and tools can help with pricing, such as price optimization software, to analyze competitive prices and for customer relationship management (CRM).

6. Monitor the effects and make necessary adjustments

At the very end, there must be monitoring of results. It's essential to track sales, margins, and customer behavior to see how your new pricing strategy is impacting your business. Otherwise, you will have no idea what effect you achieved at all.

Combining strategies

Of course, you don't have to stick to just one pricing strategy. On the contrary, in many cases, it's worth mixing and matching pricing strategies and tactics to find the right combination for your business.

The key to success is understanding the strengths and weaknesses of each strategy, and how they can be used together to create a comprehensive plan.

For example, you might use higher pricing when introducing a new product and then switch to penetration pricing once you've gained market share.

You can also use a value-based pricing strategy (or prestige pricing) for some products and services and a competitive pricing strategy for others. Then, from time to time, you can use psychological pricing (package or discount pricing).

It's important to experiment and find the right combination of pricing strategies and tactics that work best for your business.

Developing and implementing an effective retail pricing strategy is essential for any business that wants to succeed in today's competitive marketplace. There is no one-size-fits-all pricing strategy, so you'll need to take the time to understand your business, your customers, and your competition before creating a strategy that's right for you.

3

Building a Strong Foundation for Your Business

The wholesale business has its specifics that need to be taken into account at the start. More often than not, the clients of such companies are other companies, and the amount of initial investment depends on the chosen scheme. We tell you how to start working in the wholesale business

The essence of such a business is to purchase large quantities at a lower cost and sell them in small wholesale with your margin. You can get by with small investments if you do not purchase goods, but agree to their sale.

Another option is to rent a warehouse, purchase, and find a buyer for the existing goods. This will require start-up capital, but due to the speed of sales of wholesale quantities, it will be quickly returned.

Advantages of wholesale business

The balance in the domestic market depends on the B2B sector. The efficiency of a wholesale business is almost always higher than that of a retail business, due to the large assortment and high turnover.

Main advantages of wholesale business:

1. Big deals.
2. Extensive sales geography.
3. Relatively low marketing costs.

How to understand what to trade in the wholesale business

For wholesale sales, you can organize direct delivery of goods to customers or rent a warehouse. In working according to the first scheme, there are no costs for maintaining a warehouse, but the second scheme is more popular.

To decide which industry to work in, it is worth conducting a market analysis. It will help you understand which products are best to sell. When choosing products for wholesale sales, it is important to consider the following factors:

In which region will the business be organized? For example, purchasing products from local manufacturers is cheaper than importing goods from other regions or abroad.

What is the market capacity? It is important to determine whether the market is overcrowded with the product you are going to sell.

Will it depend on the season? All other things being equal, it is better to choose those product items that do not have seasonal fluctuations in demand.

Will it be possible to store products so that they do not spoil? You should not purchase perishable products unless there is a prior agreement with the buyer.

Will it be possible to organize logistics? For some categories of goods, there are financial risks during transportation. This applies, for example, to electronics, earthenware plumbing, and dishes.

Participants and logic of wholesale trade

The sales chain in a wholesale business includes the manufacturer, supplier, and seller. The latter receives goods from a distribution center, which may be included in the wholesaler's warehouse system. Large companies in the wholesale business purchase products directly from the manufacturer, while small ones work through a distributor.

The goods are sold wholesale through the AVLTPL chain.

A - Assortment, assortment. There are wide (> 1000 items), limited (from 200 to 1000 items), and narrow (< 200 items) assortments. Another option is a specialized assortment. It is usually purchased from dealers and distributors.

V - Volumes, volumes. The higher the volume, the higher the profit. But more investments are required, and risks also increase.

L - Logistics, logistics. Most of the money is spent on delivery, customs clearance, and storage of goods.

T - Turnover, turnover. With large volumes and low turnover, you need a large warehouse and a lot of money. The faster the goods turn around, the more the wholesaler earns. It is best to organize everything so that the goods are delivered directly from the factory to the buyer. This will allow you not to waste resources on storing products and not slow down turnover.

P - Planning, planning. If a wholesaler has a wide range of products, he can make more profit. But appropriate investments are required. Therefore, at the initial stage, it is better to sell a more limited range. To do this, you need to make a plan: where to get the goods; calculate how long it will take to sell them; prepare money for purchasing the batch; and think about where the goods will be stored before sale.

L - Loans, deferments, and loans. Time passes from the moment of purchasing a product to its sale. A business must have finances that will support operations until it makes a profit. If the chain is already debugged, the manufacturer can grant a deferred payment. A wholesaler who is confident in the buyer does the same: he ships the goods to retail with a deferred payment.

What agreement to conclude with a supplier in the field of wholesale trade

An agency agreement is concluded between an entrepreneur engaged in wholesale trade and the supplier of goods, which sets out the obligations of the parties. The terms of cooperation must be recorded in writing: sales volumes, payment methods, and deadlines.

Individuals can also engage in wholesale business. Contracts can be concluded regardless of whether you are self-employed or an individual entrepreneur.

Is it possible to start a wholesale business from scratch without large investments?

If you find a reliable supplier who is willing to deliver goods directly to the buyer, you can start a wholesale business without major investments. A scheme where a seller operates without its warehouse and enters into an agreement with a supplier for direct delivery of goods is called drop shipping. It works like this:

1. The seller accepts the order and transfers it to the supplier.
2. The seller accepts payment for the order and transfers the money to the supplier minus the commission.
3. The supplier sends the order to the buyer.

With this form of work, there is no need to rent a warehouse, purchase and store goods, or pay for the work of personnel servicing the warehouse. Investments will be required in finding and attracting clients. If the task is to do this in an online environment, then you will have to invest in the development and promotion of the site

How to open a wholesale business: instructions

First, you need to conduct a market analysis and select a niche and products for sale. Let's look at the steps that will allow you to open a wholesale business, using the example of selling food products.

We find a manufacturer. It is important to negotiate a price that is significantly lower than the price you expect to receive from the sale.

We select a warehouse. You need to consider the area, gate size, availability of necessary equipment, and other factors, depending on your product. So, there should be enough space so that you can quickly find the necessary goods and ship them without obstacles. For food products, correct storage conditions must be ensured by the requirements of the sanitary service. It is also important that the warehouse is in good transport accessibility from suppliers and buyers.

We are looking for suppliers. If you plan to purchase large quantities, it is more profitable to work with manufacturing plants. In other cases, it is worth paying attention to wholesale stores in the region. To earn a stable income while doing a wholesale business, you need to find reliable suppliers. This is important so that there are no supply interruptions and customers do not have to wait long.

We are solving the transport issue. If it is not possible to purchase a truck, for the first time you can rent, lease, or hire drivers with a personal car.

We are hiring staff. The main employee working between wholesale and retail enterprises is the sales representative. We also need drivers, forwarders, an accountant, and a warehouse manager. Qualified personnel should be sought and hired. Then you won't have to do everything yourself or spend a lot of time supervising the team.

We organize sales. The sales strategy depends on the characteristics of the product and logistics features.

How to increase sales in a wholesale business

To increase your wholesale sales one-time, you can use the following methods:

1. "cold" calling potential clients or email campaigns;
2. control of marketing expenses;
3. presentation of goods at exhibitions, conferences, and other specialized events;
4. incentives for repeated cooperation - bonuses for regular customers, information about new products, promotions;
5. attracting intermediaries to stimulate wholesale sales.

If your plans are for constant income growth, you should pay attention to systematic methods:

1. automate stages of the production process;
2. introduce a clear pricing policy and reasonably update it;
3. motivate employees - train them, stimulate them to fulfill and exceed the plan in material and intangible ways;
4. create a logistics department to optimize processes.

How to find regular customers in a wholesale business

For profits to flow continuously, it is important to constantly attract new customers. Creating a sales funnel is suitable for this:

1. First, its stages are determined and worked out.
2. Then they ensure that as many representatives of the target audience as possible get into the funnel.
3. As the results of the work appear, the funnels collect conversion data at each stage.
4. Analyze the results and make changes to the funnel if necessary.

To spend less money on marketing, you should turn existing customers into regular ones. To do this, they send out an email newsletter and introduce a loyalty program.

It is also important to work on relationships with counterparties, improve service, and set reasonable prices for your goods.

Common beginner mistakes

Wholesalers face the same problems as retail outlets. Ho,wever due to the large scale of operations, these mistakes turn out to be decisive for the existence of the business. You can't start working intuitively, without a clear plan of action, analysis, studying the target audience, and finding the right contacts.

In the wholesale business, newbie entrepreneurs usually make the following mistakes:

1. Few and ineffective interactions with counterparties.

2. They do not establish joint work between different departments of the enterprise.
3. Warehouses are managed ineffectively.
4. They poorly monitor financial flows, and as a result, they end up with cash gaps and try to eliminate them with the help of loans.

Another common mistake is improper resource allocation. For example, there is no need to invest in perishable goods and pay employees higher than market wages without forming a relationship with retail. It is better to use free finances to optimize processes and develop supply and sales channels.

You can start a wholesale business even without large investments. Whatever scheme the entrepreneur chooses, before launching, you need to prepare thoroughly. A detailed business plan with mandatory preliminary calculations of costs and expected profits will help with this.

4

Leveraging Technology and Automation

According to experts, the market for large and wholesale trade has reached maturity. Today, in a crisis, as well as increasing competition, businesses are looking for more and more opportunities to reduce costs and maintain budgets for the implementation of core activities. We decided to tell you about an effective way to effectively manage basic business processes - automation.

You can significantly reduce costs by optimizing the quantity of goods and the speed of their movement in all business chains. It will become easier to increase customer loyalty as soon as the implementation of loyalty programs and discount systems takes less time and requires fewer resources. The danger of seasonal resets due to high demand for a particular product or its excess in stock can and should be regulated and controlled. In all this, you do not forget that electronic programs help you improve the performance of both your business and your entire team.

We talked with experts, those who understand the specifics of managing large and wholesale networks and found out what automation programs exist, what problems you may encounter when implementing them, and how exactly the system will help increase your profits.

The key features of the wholesale trade market are high competition, low margins and a huge number of transactions. To achieve success in such conditions, distribution companies use all available tools and often invent new ones. From the point of view of business technology and the level of informatization, wholesale trade today occupies a leading position.

The basic component of the information infrastructure of any automated trading company is a set of systems for managing business processes: procurement and inventory, supply chains, assortment, settlements with counterparties, and so on. The first wave of automation of leading market players took place in the mid-2000s. The continued growth of competition has led to the fact that today SFA systems (Sales Force Automation, sales management system) have become a must-have not only for large and medium-sized companies. Local and regional distributors are also forced to automate. The current economic situation has led to the fact that the customer has become at the forefront - both the reseller and the final buyer. The distributor needs to keep his finger on the pulse all the time and understand all current and future problems, prevent them, and not just eliminate them.

Advantages of wholesale trade automation systems

1. Time to place an order is reduced;
2. The number of processed orders increases;
3. The costs of training employees are reduced, they get involved in

LEVERAGING TECHNOLOGY AND AUTOMATION

work much faster and do not distract colleagues;
4. Employees get the opportunity to work with tasks both offline and remotely;
5. Accounts receivable are reduced;
6. Executive discipline increases;
7. Additional motivation for employees comes;
8. The effectiveness of any marketing activities increases.

Solutions for automating the work of distribution companies make it possible to serve customers efficiently and quickly, which increases their loyalty.

One of the most important things in the automation of wholesale and large retail trade is warehouse automation. After all, a warehouse is, of course, the most important and integral part of all business processes for any trading company, regardless of whether it has its own warehouse or rents it. It is obvious that due to growing trade turnover, warehouse business processes become ineffective, lose control and directly affect the company's net profit in the absence of proper automation.

Wholesale trade companies can either simply be distributors or have their own production. In this case, we will consider warehouse automation in relation to a wholesaler-distributor or retailer, that is, companies that do not have their own production. Automation will directly ensure the uninterruptedness and speed of purchases/deliveries, which again directly affects the profit of the enterprise.

The approach to automation depends on the scale of the wholesale company, the direction of trade, the structure of the assortment, and most importantly, on the availability of its own production facilities. In a warehouse, it is important to ensure the speed of acceptance of goods into the warehouse, processing of applications from the buyer, delivery, etc., accounting software systems influence the increase in the efficiency of all these indicators. As an example, let's take data collection terminals, which make it possible to eliminate mis-grading in the warehouse, defects, etc. Today, not a single wholesale company above the average level can do without such products.

"Director of the pre-sale department, Sales Division of ATOL"

Implementation of CRM. From lead registration to deal closure

Over the past year, I have written several works that covered the issues of choosing a CRM and reviews of specific systems. But in practice, I came across another important issue on this topic, which I would like to highlight in this chapter. This is a matter of implementing a CRM system. I will specifically give a simple but practical example so that you can quickly understand the issue and use it for yourself.

This chapter will be intended to help understand the issue of implementing CRM and I hope it will be useful both to specialists who are involved in the implementation of CRM, and to those who want to implement it at home.

Where should you start implementing a CRM system?

The first place to start implementing CRM is a description of the sales business process. The description of the business process reflects the following points:

1. what are the stages of the sales process?
2. which departments and employees are involved at this or that stage of work
3. what documents are generated?
4. what events need to be created and reflected at each stage of work

That is, the business process reflects all stages of working with a client from beginning to end. Typically, a business process is described in BPMN format (a system of conventions (notation) for modeling business processes).

Sales stages in the business process of providing services

As a rule, in different service companies there is approximately the same list of stages of the sales process with minor variations. My sales process looks like this:

1. Initial contact from a potential client - the client goes to the landing page, fills out and sends the form, or calls the specified phone number, and the lead is registered in the CRM system
2. Determining the client's needs - negotiations through phone calls, email correspondence, communication via Skype, etc. in order to identify the client's need
3. Preparation of a proposal based on the information obtained at

the previous stage
4. Coordination of the proposal
5. Providing a service - this stage may include several stages. At different enterprises, these stages and their number are different depending on the specifics of the services provided by the companies
6. Closing acts and receiving feedback - signing documents based on the results of the work done

So, let's look at each stage of the business process one by one: what happens at a specific stage, how it is reflected in CRM, what settings need to be made in the system. I would like to note right away that we will not be tied to a specific CRM system, since the technical details differ in different systems, but in general the model of actions is the same.

1. Initial contact from a potential client

During the initial contact, it is necessary to collect as much information as possible about the potential client. Such information is entered into a separate type of client called Lead. Information can be filled in manually, for example, when receiving a phone call, or automatically when collecting leads from a website or landing page. It is this type of lead creation that I would like to dwell on in more detail.

The client fills out an application form (feedback, order a call) on your website or landing page. The number of fields and their contents are determined individually depending on what information about the potential client you need at this stage. The Name and Phone fields are the minimum that must be present in the application.

And at this stage, it is very important to determine where the potential client "came" from to your website or landing page. I'll tell you how I implemented this.

I place an ad in Yandex Direct or Google Adwards, for example, "Business consultant generalist." A person clicks this ad and goes to my website. When you go to a website in the address bar of your browser, the Google or Yandex system transmits the parameters where the client "came" from. In this case, I am interested in 2 parameters:

- Search engine (Google Adwards or Yandex Direct)
- The keyword by which the client found my ad (for example, a generalist business consultant)

Accordingly, when a person visits a site through a search engine, in the application form, in addition to the main fields (telephone, name, etc.), there are three hidden fields (Search engine, Keyword, Source, which is automatically filled in with the site address). The client does not know that we already have some information about him, he does not see hidden fields.

When a lead is generated in the CRM system, a task is automatically created for the user. For me it looks like this: "Call lead so-and-so at such-and-such a time." I define the call time as follows: lead registration time + 1 hour. I give myself an hour to contact a potential client. If I don't call, I constantly get a reminder about the task in the system. You can also set up emails with tasks and urgency reminders. If I don't call for a long time, I receive a notification every hour that I need to call the client.

We recorded the initial request in the CRM system. This is a lead. Next, you need to find out the client's need.

2. Finding out the client's needs

What happens at this stage? I contact a potential client by phone or email, this is reflected in the CRM system. In order for this data to be reflected in the CRM system, it is necessary to integrate the system with your account and telephony.

During the conversation with the client, he is qualified, that is, we understand whether the potential client is ready to cooperate or not. If the client is ready to discuss the terms of cooperation with you, you need to convert him to a Contact and create a Deal. Why do we convert it to Contact? This means that we can track statistics on the conversion of leads into contacts, draw conclusions about the effectiveness of work, and make management decisions.

The transaction specifies the stage "Clarification of the client's needs." Also at this stage, you can create tasks with reminders that record agreements with the client on further interactions.

3. Preparation proposals

I prepare a proposal based on how I spoke with the client in the previous step. At this stage, all correspondence, all calls for clarification should go only through the CRM system in order to clearly control the history of interactions with the client: who called, when they called, how much time was spent on the conversation, what was discussed with the client.

The Transaction establishes the "Proposal Preparation" stage. An offer can be generated directly in the CRM system. To do this, you need to enter information about the services provided into the system. When the offer is formed, it is sent to the client, this is recorded in the system.

4. Coordination of the proposal

The next stage, which is established in the Transaction, is "Agreement of the offer". After submitting the proposal, I meet with the client whenever possible. If this is not possible, I negotiate by phone, Skype, or mail. The purpose of the negotiation is to agree on the terms sent to the client at the previous stage. All interactions with the client are recorded in the system. If necessary, the proposal is revised and sent back to the client.

At this stage, we note in the Transaction the transaction amount and the approximate deadline for closing the transaction.

5. Provision of service

As I wrote above, the service provision stage may include several stages. The number and content of stages depends on the specifics of the services provided by companies. All interactions with the client at this stage are recorded in the system.

We will not consider financial issues of payment for services here. But here's what I want to draw your attention to: many clients make the mistake of believing that if the client has paid for the services or signed an agreement, the transaction has been successfully completed and can be closed. But this is not true: CRM is a customer relationship management system, not just a sales management system. And the transaction is considered successfully completed if the conditions are met on both sides, and not just payment has been received. The transaction can be closed after the provision of services and closing of acts.

6. Closing acts and receiving feedback

After the service is provided and payment is made, documentation for closing is generated, a service acceptance certificate, which is sent to the client. Next, you need to request feedback from the client about your cooperation. Receiving feedback - I myself adhere to this and implement it for my clients so that there is always a feedback, a response from the client based on the results of cooperation. After completing all stages of the work, the deal is closed (the "Closed and Won" stage is set).

What is needed to implement a CRM system?

Let me summarize what is needed to start working in a CRM system:

1. Description of the sales business process
2. Reflection of business process stages in transaction stages in CRM
3. Integration of the system with a website or landing page to collect leads
4. Setting up an email account
5. Integration of CRM with telephony

I would like to add what nuance you need to pay attention to: for all phone calls and negotiations, it is very important to have a script. A script is a sequence of actions that an employee (sales manager) must perform when negotiating with a client. The more detailed the scripts, the more advanced they are, the better. If you have a small company, the presence of scripts is not necessary; if you have a large company, this is already necessary.

Why do we need all these details, transitions from one stage to another, and recording of this data in the system? In order to clearly see the picture of the company's work, have indicators and reporting, know how many leads you convert into contacts, how many contacts you close a deal with. One of the main reports of the CRM system is the sales funnel; it is formed based on data on the stages of the transaction. This is a report that clearly displays the quantitative relationship of all transactions at different stages and allows you to plan work and make management decisions.

II

Mastering Wholesaling Techniques

5

Finding Lucrative Real Estate Deals

The question of where to invest savings always remains relevant, but especially when economic changes occur. Real estate remains one of the popular instruments in this regard residential and commercial properties remain in demand and are capable of generating good profits.

We tell you how and what kind of real estate to invest in and what you need for this.

Real Estate Investment Goals

Investing is investing money to make a profit. People invest in real estate to:

1. Get passive income. To do this, they use their vacant property, buy a new one for cash, or take out a mortgage. Then they find tenants and make a profit every month.
2. Save your savings. To prevent money from depreciating due to inflation, it is often invested in real estate. They buy commercial,

residential, budget, and luxury premises. Those that will not go down in price. It is better to buy commercial properties in areas with high traffic, and residential ones in areas with developing infrastructure.
3. Receive income from resale or exchange at a premium.

Pros and cons of investing in real estate

There is always a demand for real estate, but not every property is profitable to invest in. Let's figure out what the advantages and disadvantages of investing in real estate are.

pros

- **Stability**. Residential and commercial premises, when properly selected, are in demand.
- **Passive income.** It doesn't take much effort to make a profit from a purchased apartment.
- **Minimal risks**. Even during a crisis, real estate can be sold or rented out.
- **Rising prices.** Real estate is not affected by inflation, just like gold. The cost is only increasing.
- **Multiple investment options**. There are different options for how to make a profit: rent out daily or for a long time, resell, divide into small segments, and others.

Cons

- **High price**. To purchase real estate you need an impressive amount.
- **Long payback period**. Real estate will begin to generate income

above its cost in 5-10 years.
- **Additional expenses**. This includes utilities, major repairs, and a tax of 13% of the transaction amount.

What kind of real estate can you invest in?

The larger the city, the higher the demand for residential and commercial space. Let's consider investment options.

Residential Properties.

The most common type of real estate. Mostly new investors work with it since the risks are minimal. This type of investment is often used to save money. Income is received through resale or rental. When purchasing a residential property, take into account all the characteristics: location, year of construction, layout, and infrastructure.

Commercial real estate

Suitable for investors with experience - it is easier for them to choose suitable premises. It is more profitable to rent out commercial real estate than to resell it.

Land

Buying land plots is profitable because they are cheaper than other types of real estate. They are quick and easy to apply for. There are no additional costs in the form of utility bills and repairs. When purchasing, consider the purpose. The most liquid are plots for construction. Agricultural land is suitable for long-term investment.

Country estate

Country houses as a type of investment are especially popular among residents of megacities. There will be a stable demand for comfortable houses with beautiful views and nature around.

New buildings at the foundation pit stage

Developers set minimum prices to "pump up" demand and attract buyers' attention to the property at the initial stage of construction. Buyers of apartments at this stage will have to wait longer than others, and the developer will compensate for this inconvenience using the price factor.

Investments in parking spaces

Situational type of investment in large cities. Income depends on the location of the site. The parking lot is located in a busy place where there are not enough free spaces for cars.

How risky is it to invest in real estate?

Investing always involves risks, and the real estate industry is no exception. Let's look at the sources of risk.

Poor location

The investor expects that the area he has chosen will be developed and prices will rise. If this does not happen, there is no demand for the property and the owner does not make a profit.

Force mature

If the environmental situation around the facility deteriorates sharply, this will lead to a drop in demand and cost.

Unscrupulous tenants. Sometimes employers delay monthly payments or damage furniture. For repairs after such tenants need a round sum.

Depreciation

Over time, the value of objects decreases in value. For example, if a new building goes up next to a once-promising building, the apartments in it will be higher in price and more attractive to tenants.

Construction freeze

To avoid the risk of investing in housing under construction and receiving it much later than the promised date, choose accredited developers.

Fraud

There are a lot of deception schemes in the real estate industry: shell companies, selling other people's property using forged documents, and others. A legal review of real estate will help secure the transaction.

Ways to invest in real estate

There are two main ways to generate income from real estate: rental and resale at a premium.

Renting and resale have many variations, so let's look at them separately.

Rental

Apartment for long-term rent. Plus, it's an easy way to earn income, since there are always people willing to rent an apartment. It is enough to find bona fide long-term tenants, enter into an agreement, and make a profit every month. The downside is that finding good tenants can be time-consuming. In addition, this method has a low-profit margin. If you purchased an apartment as an investment, then you will not soon recoup your investment. Taking out a mortgage for a long-term rental is also unprofitable: income will not cover loan payments.

Daily apartment rental. Plus - the opportunity to make money quickly. If the yield from long-term rentals is within 5%, then for daily rentals it is up to 30%. The downside is labor costs. You will have to move in and out of tenants and clean the apartment every day. There is also a risk of damage to furniture and unplanned expenses for repairs.

Renting a cottage or country house. Plus - high income and demand. Especially during the New Year, May and summer holidays. There is also an option to divide the house in half if it is large. You can live in one half yourself and rent out the other half. The downside is unscrupulous tenants who can damage not only the furniture but also the cottage itself.

Construction of an apartment building and rental of apartments. Plus - if the constructed apartment building has a favorable location, then you will quickly rent out all the apartments. The payback period for the project is two years, then net profit. The downside is that you need start-up capital, a competent business project, and a plot of land for construction.

Renting a garage or parking space. Plus, the investment does not require large investments. The downside is low profitability. To make a profit, you need to buy several garages or parking spaces.

Resale

Purchasing housing during construction. Plus - if you buy real estate at the excavation stage, you will save up to 30% of the average market cost of housing. The downside is that you have to wait for construction to be completed. Also, some developers may indicate in their DDU that upon sale, the developer's permission for assignment is required. In rare cases, the developer may generally refuse his consent to the assignment.

Resale of land. Plus, you just need to purchase a plot and wait for the market price to rise. The land does not require additional investment or maintenance. The downside is that sometimes you have to wait for years.

Buying a home in poor condition. Plus - big profits. You buy a home cheaply, invest 200,000 rubles in repairs, and sell it for 2 times more expensive. The downside is that it takes a lot of time to find and repair such an apartment.

Procedure for investing in real estate

For investments to generate income, follow the algorithm:

1. Study the situation on the market - what kind of real estate is in demand, what buyers are looking for, what are the average prices for properties, where there are interesting locations or areas with developing infrastructure.
2. Ensure the reliability of sellers, developers, tenants, and intermediaries. Check documentation, reviews, ratings, and reputation. Look for any legal disputes or downtime.
3. Select a liquid item to purchase.

Overall, the real estate industry is stable. With the right approach, even a beginner will increase his capital.

How to make more money in real estate

There are several ways to increase the return on investment several times.

You are dividing a large apartment into studios. It is more profitable to rent an apartment to several tenants. For example, you rent out a three-room apartment for 40,000 rubles. If you divide it into three one-room apartments and take 20,000 rubles from each tenant, you will receive 60,000 rubles.

Redevelopment. This method allows not only to improve living conditions but also to increase the value of real estate by 30–40%. Please note that any redevelopment must be coordinated with the BTI and changes must be made to the technical passport.

Expansion of premises due to completion. If you add a balcony, veranda, or basement to a property, its value will immediately increase by 20–30%.

Transfer of premises from residential to non-residential and vice versa. Purchasing commercial real estate requires a large investment. The solution is to purchase housing on the ground floor of an apartment building, and then transfer it to non-residential use.

High-quality repairs. Repairs increase the cost of an apartment by 1.5-2 times. For example, an apartment in poor condition costs 3 million, you made repairs for 500 thousand rubles - now the price can be increased to 5 million.

6

10 Ways to Motivate Employees

How to force employees to work if they don't want to? No way. There is no point in forcing - you need to find out what motivates the people on your team, for what they are willing to move mountains. And then they will have both desire and energy. Each team has its motivators, I have calculated 10 universal methods. They require virtually no investment but significantly increase the productivity of staff. I share them with you.

1. Renaming the position

It's good when the job title reflects the essence of the work, but it's even better if it gives the person a certain social status. Do you know the expression "Whatever you call a ship, that's how it will sail"? So, this rule also works in motivation.

The most striking example: not everyone will proudly tell family and friends that they work as a cleaner, although this work is as respected as any other. This is where the simplest method of motivation comes from - renaming the position.

So, we change the position of "cleaner/cleaning lady" in the staffing table to: "cleaning master", "cleaning specialist", "cleaning manager", "complex work foreman", and "cleanliness manager". The essence of the work does not change, but the status of its performer in the eyes of others increases, and the employee's attitude towards his tasks changes.

Or, for example, a manager is a widespread and therefore partially impersonal and devalued position. Or maybe: "project manager", "project manager", or "assistant manager for customer service".

How to involve employees in the process of renaming positions

1. Let each of them think about the meaning and benefit of his work.
2. He will "stand apart" from others and find what he does better than others.
3. Come up with several options for job titles and send them to management for approval.

The positive effect of this method begins to be felt from the moment a new job title is invented: a person becomes involved, "refreshes" his attitude towards work, and again formulates tasks and meanings for himself.

2. Team spirit

The atmosphere in the team, and team spirit - these are things that cannot be measured and counted, but they greatly influence the company's efficiency. This is communication between employees and at the "manager-subordinate" level. Work will be better if the relationship is friendly and built on mutual respect and trust (but without familiarity). Here are some ways to do this.

✓ **Team building**

What can be team building? Various games, quests, and other activities require the team to solve puzzles together, get out of difficult situations, and simply have fun and relax. As a rule, after such events the work process goes better - employees get to know each other and establish mutual assistance.

✓ **Team meetings**

It is advisable to hold regular meetings - not only in critical situations but also when you simply need to discuss something relevant. Praise people openly, express gratitude to them, and talk about successful deals and prospects. It motivates.

✓ **Personal conversation**

If we talk about communication between a manager and a subordinate, personal conversation and feedback bring people closer together and help them quickly achieve company and personal goals. If you are a boss, try to communicate with employees not only about work topics but also about others. Help me grow. Be a little more than just a boss for them, find out more about them, and take an interest in their affairs, only then will you feel the impact.

3. Comfort

On job search sites, you often find employer advertisements that indicate "a cozy office with a coffee machine and cookies." This is not a fancy word. People care about comfort and having a good time in the office.

✓ Lighting, temperature

Perhaps you haven't paid much attention to whether there is a lamp at each workplace and how different points of the office are generally illuminated. This is very important for employees who work late and with short daylight hours in winter.

Check how the workplaces are located: quite often there is a problem in offices - while some are comfortable with the air conditioner on or an open window, others are freezing sitting directly in the airflow. "Climate wars" do not add motivation - ensure that the temperature in the office is acceptable for everyone.

✓ Convenient workplace

Repair or replace a chair that is not height adjustable. Separate your desk with a partition if you have a call center. It doesn't matter what field you work in - manufacturing, medicine, beauty - as a rule, people spend at least 8 hours "on duty", and the workspace should help them, and not add discomfort.

✓ Healthy food

If possible, provide people with healthy food. You can order food delivery to your office or pay for business lunches in the cafe opposite. Taking care of your health and such a pleasant bonus will inspire employees of any level.

4. Training

Training motivates employees, prevents professional burnout, and allows them to maintain interest in the profession for a long time. How can you not take advantage of such benefits? Moreover, some of the types of training are free or conditionally free:

- specialized electronic literature;
- webinars;
- mentoring;
- discussions at specially designated times to discuss professional issues.

If your budget allows, include online courses and training in your program.

5. Career growth

Not all people want to move up the career ladder - this requires responsibility, high levels of commitment, and long working hours. Others want but are not up to the task. To ensure that expectations and reality coincide and that both the company and employees achieve their goals, it is necessary to draw up a career plan for each employee and supervise his professional activities.

The subordinate must understand: that it is impossible to come to work as a consultant, and a month later take the position of a boss. A career is built progressively and depends on many factors. But a manager can set a lower, but still good, bar for a potential manager: discuss the opportunity to become a senior manager, then a supervisor of newcomers, a mentor. And if certain conditions are met - as a leader. With this approach, a person receives personal development, communication skills, and status as a bonus.

Companies are interested in employees becoming better because professionalism directly affects the profitability of the business. So train your people. And, by the way, do not forget that a career can develop not only vertically, but also horizontally - a company does not need an endless number of managers, but strong experts in their field are always needed.

6. Non-standard nominations

How do you reward the best employees? The status of "Best Manager" sounds nice, but hackneyed. A good option is to collectively come up with a list of non-standard nominations, for example:

- consummate salesman;
- office fairy;
- reception shower;
- profitable manager;
- brilliant accountant;
- wizard of finance;
- career predictor;
- phenomenal extra;
- planetary guide to abilities.

At the end of the month, quarter, or year, choose the best by secret ballot and publish a corporate newspaper or newsletter with photos of the winners. Reward employees, not with money, but with gifts, for example: dinner for two in a restaurant, theater tickets, a gym membership, and a certificate for visiting an SPA salon.

An important point: nominations should only be positive and awarded fairly.

7. Gamification

Gamification unites the team, increases interest in daily work, makes relationships in the team warm and friendly, quickly adapts newcomers to work, and allows for training in a non-standard form.

I'll tell you the three stages in which this tool is implemented.

1) Identifying the need for motivation. It is determined which pain points need to be closed, and which are not satisfactory in the work.

2) Development of a motivation system. Points A and B are determined, and a path is built between them, focusing on the specifics of the business, the company's goals, and the characteristics of the employees.

3) Testing the process and receiving feedback from the team. Next comes analysis of the results, making adjustments, and global implementation into the business.

8. Balance

In 2020, a study was conducted on the compatibility of work and personal life. The worst at this are doctors (39%), marketing managers (40%), sales managers, PR managers, and executives (41% each).

It's clear with doctors: shift work, night shifts, emergency jobs, a pandemic, but why did managers get here? Most likely, because the manager's salary depends on the result. To ensure high performance, people are forced to give up weekends, vacations, and sick leave. "Expectation of sales" also hurts the human psyche, which leads to burnout and staff turnover. However, it is up to the manager to structure the work process so that it does not interfere with his personal life.

What is important to today's employees

1) Young people do not want to "die at work" even for big money. Priorities have changed: between salary and atmosphere in the company, they choose the latter. And they will be right: money is not worth lost health, because everything you earn will then have to be spent on treatment and recovery.

2) The following phrases are often found in vacancies: friendly staff, a young creative team, adequate management, and corporate events. And it motivates. A person wants to feel like a member of a team and not a cog in a machine. Warm, friendly relationships in the team help maintain a balance between work and personal life and provide confidence in the future.

9. Gratitude

If you want to motivate your staff to achieve results, don't skimp on gratitude. There are lots of ways to do this unusually.

10 Free Ways to Say Thank You

1. Record a video thank you to the employee who showed the best result in sales
2. Allow him to come to work later than usual or, conversely, leave

earlier than the rest if the manager fulfills the plan.
3. Invite to participate in a meeting on a difficult issue.
4. Call your subordinate in the morning, praise him, and wish him a good day.
5. Go into the accounting department, office, commercial department, and other departments of your company without any reason - take a sincere interest in the affairs of their employees.
6. Assign your best employee as a mentor.
7. Take a photo together with a colleague who made a profitable deal, and place the photo on the "honor board".
8. Thank the employee for a good job. Without any reason or connection to the holidays.
9. Offer to take you home in your company car.
10. Allow no dress code on Fridays.

10. Humanity

Be flexible. Do not punish a person with a fine if he is late for work by a few minutes - situations vary. And if this is an isolated case, be loyal. "Legalize" 15-minute tea breaks so that people can switch gears and relax. If the manager fulfills the plan and shows excellent results, do not be afraid to encourage him: allow him to leave early on Friday without loss of salary, and add paid days to his vacation. If there are women with children in the company, do not force them to beg you on their knees for two hours to go to the matinee. Of course, moderation is necessary for everything, but if a person knows that, if necessary, he can always help his loved ones by taking a few hours, then his work will be calmer. And they will treat you better.

Teaching people to love their jobs is an art. It is within the power of every manager to ensure that employees do not start waiting for Friday on Monday, but strive every day to do better results than yesterday.

7

Promotion Of Wholesale Sales

Wholesale trade is a special form of relationship between business entities, within which the parties independently form connections regarding the supply of products. Buyers purchase products for subsequent resale or professional use. Promotion of wholesale sales is required both by beginning entrepreneurs who have only recently entered the market and do not have established relationships with suppliers, and by experienced companies wishing to reach a new level.

Specifics of Wholesale Sales

Wholesale sales belong to the B2B market; goods are most often purchased in large quantities. The need for the functioning of the wholesale sales sector is due to the production needs of B2B market participants and the fact that manufacturers do not have the opportunity to directly sell goods to all consumers (except handicrafts).

When conducting wholesale activities, the coverage area is more extensive than during retail sales. An entrepreneur does not need to focus on equipping and decorating an office, looking for warehouses with advantageous locations, or thoroughly working out advertising. At the same time, the transaction amounts are significantly higher than in retail.

Wholesale participants:

1. **wholesale suppliers.** They play the role of intermediaries between producers and end consumers. Engaged in purchasing, warehousing, and marketing of products;
2. **Manufacturers.** They can also act as wholesale suppliers;
3. **Wholesalers call themselves manufacturers.** They order production of products from enterprises but sell them under their brand.

Some companies simultaneously sell products wholesale and retail. If the sales strategy is built correctly, such companies receive stable profits.

Forms of wholesale trade:

1. **Transit.** Products are supplied directly from the manufacturer to wholesale organizations or retail chains, bypassing intermediary wholesalers;
2. **Warehouse** The company supplies products to the warehouse of a wholesale company. Here it is redistributed through various distribution channels.

In both cases, marketing and activities aimed at its practical implementation play an important role.

Wholesale Sales Indicators

Entrepreneurs primarily focus on the growth of three indicators:

1. **Turnover**
2. **Margins**
3. **Profitability**

There are several other indicators that business owners should pay attention to:

1. **Average Check.** Shows the average amount of goods customers buy;
2. **Conversion Rate.** Shows what percentage of users out of the total number of site visitors completed the target action;
3. Number of transactions per client for a certain period (month, year);
4. The number of potential buyers for a certain period;
5. Other indicators (based on the specifics of the company's activities).

The more key indicators a business owner analyzes, the clearer the picture he sees. Using them, you can formulate an effective strategy for increasing wholesale sales.

How can a wholesale company attract large customers

A wholesale buyer differs from a retail buyer in that he is well aware of the characteristics of the product, its advantages and disadvantages. For him, the most important thing is ease of purchase and high speed of delivery. From this, we can conclude that to attract wholesalers it is necessary to create a website with special features.

Unfortunately, many online stores do not have a wholesale section. Because of this, a potential buyer is forced to call the company with a request to send him a price list. As a result, he has to wait until the manager downloads the data from the 1C program makes a table in Excel, and then sends the file by email.

During this time, impatient customers have time to study competitors' websites and place an order from them. Therefore, if a business owner wants to take a step towards meeting wholesale customers, he must provide the ability to download a price list directly from the website. Today, suppliers are chosen not only by price level but also by the level of service offered.

When is it necessary to take measures to promote wholesale sales?

Promotion will be required in the following cases:

- Competitors dump prices;
- Managers often break deals;
- Buyers choose only those products that have the lowest prices. And at the same time, they are negotiating for prices to become even

lower;
- Clients constantly ask for deferred payments and do not transfer money on time.

A young business that has not yet worked with anyone on the market and has not had time to develop a reputation needs promotion.

Standard methods of promoting wholesale sale

Various methods are used to sell products in the wholesale industry. Some allow you to quickly sell a batch of goods, while others provide a systemic effect.

Cold Calls

The idea is to call potential clients with whom the company has never worked before. The method has a drawback: a potential client may refuse to conduct telephone conversations with the manager of a company unknown to him. The chances of success will increase if, before making calls, you draw up a portrait of a potential client and determine his needs, and then, based on this information, create an offer that the client cannot refuse.

Cold calling will be most effective if the company owner creates a systematic sales department with its plans, metrics, scripts, etc. If you assign ordinary managers to make calls, the results will be minimal. To track the sales process in the department, it is necessary to implement a CRM system.

Industry Exhibitions

At such events, companies present their products, find potential customers, and exchange contacts with them. To become a participant in the exhibition, you need to set up a stand, communicate with visitors, and offer them products. Participation in events of this level helps a business create a positive image.

We need to work with the contacts collected at exhibitions. It makes no sense to sit and wait for clients to call. It's better to call first remind yourself about yourself, and try to start a dialogue. If you don't do this, people will simply forget about your company.

Creation of a website for wholesale trade

A wholesale online store can be created from scratch or based on a ready-made solution. It will fulfill several purposes at once: attract the attention of potential customers, provide information about products and the company, collect contacts, and sell products. It is important that the website contains complete and reliable information about the products and includes photographs. If the client does not find the information he is interested in, he will leave the site and go to competitors.

Newsletters by Emails

Newsletters help retain and return customers and attract leads. They can also help create an image of an expert and help people understand the properties of products. Contacts are taken from our database. You can sell through a newsletter in two ways: warming up with content or directly offering to purchase goods. The effectiveness of email campaigns is monitored using a CRM system.

Communication on Specialized sites

The target audience of a wholesale business can be present on specialized portals, forums, and message boards. When choosing a profile site, you need to ensure that it is related to the chosen area of activity. For example, in a forum, sellers can discuss everyday problems associated with running a business, and a representative from a wholesale company will offer them a solution or give valuable advice.

It is important to maintain a dialogue on the site on an ongoing basis. Just registering is not enough, you need to be active. You should not expect an immediate effect; results will appear only over time.

Hiring a manager with an Established Client Base

A customer base is a useful tool, the use of which can help increase sales volumes and acquire regular customers. If an entrepreneur has not yet managed to develop his client base, he can hire a manager who has already managed to develop one. True, strategically for business this is not the most interesting option, since the manager may begin to set his conditions or will easily leave you for another company.

Wholesale Marketing

Promotion of wholesale sales is based on the use of various tools and methods to convey to customers information about the advantages of products and the benefits of purchasing from a specific supplier, as well as to make potential customers want to purchase them. The seller conveys messages to his target audience through marketing communications.

Basic ways to promote wholesale sales:

1. **Advertising.** It is used more often than other methods. The advertising message focuses on the quality characteristics of the goods and the benefits of purchasing from a particular company;
2. **Personal Selling.** Based on direct contact between the seller and the potential client. May take the form of business negotiations;
3. **Sales Promotion.** It consists of implementing incentive measures to encourage purchases. The emphasis is on providing favorable terms of cooperation;
4. **Public Relations.** The objective of the method is to create a favorable image of the company with the help of the media and disseminate commercially important information about it.

In addition to the basic methods of promotion, auxiliary marketing technologies are also used: direct marketing, online promotion, exhibition and fair activities, etc. The choice of promotion method depends on the personal preferences of the company's management. In recent years, the promotion of goods in the Internet environment has been gaining popularity among companies operating in the field of wholesale sales.

Advertising costs can account for up to 20% of a company's revenue, so careful analysis of its effectiveness is necessary. By eliminating ineffective activities, the business will save a large amount of money.

Working with the client-based

It is easier for a company to sell products to those customers who have already bought something from it than to attract new ones. In this case, the condition must be met: the client received decent service and was satisfied with the cooperation. To achieve maximum impact, managers need to move away from using Excel spreadsheets and notepads. Instead, you need to work with a CRM system and use other online tools.

Drawing up a portrait of an ideal client

Business owners have probably heard about the need to create a portrait of an ideal client, but only a few do this. The basis is taken as a buyer with whom the business has been working for a long time and who is satisfied with everything. All offers, marketing policies, and work of the company should be tailored to this client.

The audience needs to be segmented, but the "everything for everyone" approach will not bring the desired results. It makes no sense to invest time and resources in buyers and at the same time achieve minimal income (or even negative income).

Building Relationships

Today people receive a large flow of information from all sides and because of this they can quickly forget about you. To prevent this from happening, you need to regularly remind yourself. Several communication channels are used at once. They start by sending newsletters containing information about profitable discounts, special offers, product range updates, and useful tips.

In addition to sending newsletters, you need to regularly call your regular customers and ask them what's going on now, how things are going, etc. You can schedule calls in a CRM system. It is also necessary to periodically hold meetings with clients.

Development of individual pricing policy

Buyers will appreciate the opportunity to receive discounts and bonuses; such measures can tie them to you for a long time. The chances that they will continue to buy products from you increase significantly. Clients also love deferred payments; sometimes without this, it is difficult for a business to establish cooperation. When developing a pricing policy, you need to look at how beneficial such measures are to the company itself.

Increasing the level of service

Some domestic entrepreneurs neglect service, which is why it can be considered a competitive advantage. Companies offering a high level of service stand out from their competitors.

To increase customer loyalty, a business owner must ensure the following:

1. **Getting quick access to the current assortment.** This is very important for potential clients because then they will not have to waste time calling managers and finding out whether the required product items are available. And if the goods need to be urgently delivered somewhere, the client will choose a competitor whose product range is publicly available. The optimal solution is to

create a personal account on the website for all clients;

2. **Emphasis not only on low price but also on the convenience of the target audience.** It is important to meet delivery deadlines. If a company promises to deliver a product within three days, this condition must be met. Otherwise, clients will lose trust. Some potential clients look at what work schedule the company adheres to and whether it works on weekends;

3. **Providing feedback.** Analysis of messages from customers contains the potential for the development of wholesale sales. Criticism must also be taken into account because if you eliminate factors that the client does not like, he will buy goods from you. Feedback will be most effective if you ask clients to answer questions like "Why did you choose our company?", "Why did you decide to stop working with us?";

4. **Manager involvement.** Managers must respond quickly to messages and calls. It is unlikely that a client will want to cooperate with you if he has to wait two days for a manager's response, and no one answered his call to the office. The client may not like the service or prices, but if managers show real involvement and willingness to help, the person will most likely choose to cooperate with your company.

What should a website be like to promote wholesale trade?

The most convenient and simplest option is to create an online store where only goods will be sold at wholesale prices. You can also create a "double" online store for retail and wholesale sales, using a single product database. For all products, different prices are indicated for individual customer groups. However promoting a "double" online store is more difficult, since when going to the site, wholesale customers may get confused and not immediately understand that goods are sold here at wholesale prices. Therefore, mixing wholesale and retail is not recommended.

The website must include prominent information that it specializes in wholesale sales. For this purpose, an advertising slogan, logo, and design elements are used. To automatically filter out users from non-target audiences, you can make the price list available only after registration. Having a personal account will make life much easier for clients and simplify paperwork.

The catalog must have a convenient structure; the division of products into categories is mandatory. Top products and bestsellers are displayed in a separate section; customers will pay attention to them. It is recommended to highlight narrowly niche and unique products.

If the site contains a large database of products, you will need an adequately functioning search system based on various parameters (name, article number, etc.). A nice bonus will be the presence of auto-suggestions in the search.

The ordering procedure should be simple and fast. You can add a quick order function, then regular customers will not have to constantly search for products in the catalog to add to the "Cart". Wholesalers are unlikely to be interested in loud texts and bright photographs; they look at the technical characteristics of the product.

A description of the terms of purchase, delivery, and payment should be posted on the wholesale sales website. An additional advantage will be the presence of an online calculator and an interactive price list, showing price changes depending on order volumes.

Another important point is the ability to pay for goods in different ways: using bank cards and payment systems, cash on delivery. Product items presented on the website must be in stock in the stated quantities. Errors and inconsistencies will only cause negativity on the part of customers and will lead to the loss of potential revenue in much greater quantities than in retail.

Bonus systems, cumulative discounts, and promotions will help turn visitors into regular customers. They tie them to the site and encourage them to buy even more products.

The site needs to publish information that will interest customers and benefit them. For example, the results of your research, successful cases, and tips for increasing sales.

How to promote a wholesale website

Simply creating a website and placing products on it is not enough. It is necessary to promote it in search engines and set up channels for attracting visitors. Today you can often encounter situations where companies that do not pay attention to the creation and promotion of a website suffer losses and curtail their activities.

The advantage of attracting customers using a website is that people find your company themselves. Managers do not need to impose themselves on them and offer something, as is the case with cold calls. Website promotion is carried out using keywords, advertising on social networks, and contextual advertising.

Promotion by Keywords

To quickly secure it in the top positions of search engines, you need to add the words "wholesale", "wholesale", and "wholesale" to the name of the goods. The site will be promoted for low-competition and low-frequency queries, and the percentage of targeted traffic will be higher compared to promotion for high-frequency queries. It is not recommended to promote an online store for general queries (for example, "buy cement"), as this will attract untargeted traffic in the form of retail buyers who will not be able to purchase anything.

Contextual Advertising

The promotion method helps to quickly attract customers. The first buyers will come within a few hours after the launch of the advertising campaign. The results of promotion are difficult to predict, since the traffic received may become a short-term phenomenon or provide an influx of regular customers. It is important to be able to set up contextual advertising, otherwise the business will waste its advertising budget.

Even if people don't buy anything on the site, they will learn about the supplier and the terms of cooperation offered. In the B2B sphere, suppliers are selected taking into account the company's reputation, attractiveness of purchasing, and delivery conditions. Using a website, you can convey the company's benefits to potential clients.

Social Media

Social networks advertise on a pay-per-impression and pay-per-click basis. You can also create a company community and post information about products, promotions, etc. there. This type of promotion is cheaper than contextual advertising. But to get an effect, you need to know your audience and their interests well.

The disadvantage of this method is that customers will come as long as they pay for advertising. After the advertising campaign is closed, the number of requests will decrease sharply.

8

Working with Objections in Sales- How to do it professionally

Objection handling is an important part of the sales process, where sales reps address all of a prospect's objections to move them further down the sales funnel. Objection handling must be done correctly without infuriating potential clients.

Some sales representatives become defensive and tend to argue when confronted with an objection. Because of this, they lose the deal.

When dealing with objections, sales representatives must be calm and polite. Listening is an important skill needed to convey objections. Sales reps must understand the customer's concerns and then find a middle ground that benefits both.

Common sales objections and how to deal with them

Handling objections effectively can bring you closer to your sales goals. Here are the most common objections that block the path to success for sales professionals:

1. The price is too high

No matter what you sell, there is a high chance that you will encounter buyers who have problems with the price of the product. Well, no one likes to waste their precious dollars.

Most sales reps immediately lower the price or offer a discount when a customer objects to the price. But this is like compromising the company's profits.

How to deal with this objection?

1. Instead of taking the easy route, try to be creative in demonstrating the value of your product;
2. Create a connection between price and value; you need to reasonably justify the price of your product;
3. Give examples of your satisfied customers and explain how your product helped solve a specific problem.

2. We need to consult

"I will consult with my boss/partner and get back to you." In most cases, such prospects never return. This is simply a delaying tactic used by most uninterested prospects. Don't fall into the trap and wait for them.

How to deal with this objection?

1. Try to organize a joint meeting with both parties;
2. Ask them if they can connect you directly with the decision-maker;
3. Offer them a situation like "If your partner asked you to decide at all, what would you do"?

3. Send me some information

This is the most common excuse potential clients use to avoid a conversation. Sometimes you don't even have the opportunity to present your product's value proposition or ask follow-up questions.

Don't just send the information and walk away from the deal. Take ownership of the situation and make sure your potential seller doesn't hang up on you before answering vital questions.

How to deal with this objection?
Be polite and respond:

1. - "I would be happy to send the information by email, but before doing so, I suggest taking a couple of minutes to discuss your current business challenges";
2. - "Yes, of course, but before that, do you mind if I ask you a few questions to understand how we are called to help you improve your process."

4. There's no need now

It's human nature that most people don't seek change until they're faced with a serious problem. Few businesses are so happy with their current operations that they are not willing to try something new.

Take them out of their comfort zone and show them the bigger picture. Make them realize the profits they are missing out on by not embracing change.

How to deal with this objection?

1. Give examples of clients who have made similar changes that you propose;
2. Mention the benefits that clients received from the positive change;
3. Show them what problems they will face in the future if they do not respond now.

5. "We are already working with … (your competitor)"

You may encounter companies that are already using your competitor's product. However, this does not mean that you cannot attract their attention to your product. There is a possibility that they may be dissatisfied with the product or not ready to switch and adopt the product of a new supplier.

How to deal with this objection?

1. Find the gap between the two products and sow a seed of doubt in the mind of a potential client;

2. Point out the unique advantages of your product that competitors do not have;

- if you have a client who has already used this particular competitor's product, provide an example.

Best Practices for Handling Sales Objections

Don't panic or give up when objections come your way. Stay calm, determined, and optimistic to successfully close the sale. Here are the best practices you should follow when dealing with objections.

1. Establish good relationships

Instead of being defensive when a potential client objects, try to understand them:

1. Listen carefully to their objections;
2. Make them comfortable so that they can freely share all their concerns;
3. Sometimes potential clients hide real concerns and use some excuses to avoid conversation;
4. So, connect with your potential client on an individual level and create a good relationship.

2. Dig Deeper and Explore Objections

Get more information about your prospect's objections by asking open-ended questions. Most sales professionals are uncomfortable asking prospects questions when they raise objections.

Don't be shy to ask potential clients questions. Questions are the only way to understand what is stopping your customers from buying your product. Ask them to clarify their objections.

3. Get more clarity

Sometimes it becomes difficult to understand the real problem that is preventing you from making a purchasing decision. Often sales professionals make guesses and get into trouble. Don't assume anything in sales and don't overcomplicate it. When in doubt, clarify the objection to make sure you understand the main point. Be direct and clear.

Sometimes clarification can save you from disastrous results. So, discuss and clarify with confidence.

4. Write it down or write down a sales objection.

Your potential clients may have several objections. In this case, you need to either write them down or write them down so as not to miss a single objection:

1. It is best to use a CRM with a built-in virtual phone system ;
2. By doing this, you will have all the details of the upcoming transaction during communication with the client;
3. You can easily take notes or record a call to track objections;
4. When you have objections, prioritize and resolve the objections one by one.

5. Prepare and get better.

Gather the sales team and discuss customer objections. Although your target audience is the same, every entrepreneur will have different objections. So, make a list of objections that your teammates often encounter. Find ways to deal with these objections.

Conduct test calls with your department manager and prepare to handle complex sales objections. Ask other teammates to pay attention during mock calls and offer suggestions for how to respond to objections.

6. Pause and then speak carefully.

Handling objections should be done with a calm mind. Don't respond to an objection right away. Pause, think, and choose your words carefully. Unsuccessful salespeople tend to interrupt prospects while they are talking. They speak quickly without thinking and make rash decisions, which is why they fail to convert a prospect into a paying customer.

Dealing with sales objections is the equivalent of playing chess: you have to think critically or you will lose. So take some time to think about the objection, and then respond.

7. Explain how your solution helped others.

When a potential client objects, don't get defensive. Instead, try to be polite and earn their trust. Convince them that you are sincerely interested in helping them. Give your potential clients real-life examples.

Explain how your solution helped a client solve a similar problem that the prospect is currently facing. Share case studies to build trust.

8. Select your preferred follow-up time

Clients often ask for more time to think. Give them the time they need to think about your decision. However, ask about the preferred time to call or email potential clients. Follow-up is critical in sales.

Without support, it is difficult to close a deal. If you put off the conversation, there is a chance that the deal could slip away. So don't delay this for too long, check in a few days and conclude.

Objecting to a sale is one of the most difficult parts of the sales process. However, most of the top performers made it through and moved the deal to the closing stage.

Nothing is impossible if you stay focused. Continue to improve and find new ways to handle sales objections.

III

Scaling Your Wholesaling Business

9

Scale up and maximize profits: Using CRM to Grow your Business

In today's business environment, where the pace of development and competitive pressure are extremely high, businesses are looking for effective tools to scale their operations and achieve greater success. One of the key tools that prove useful in this process is business CRM systems.

CRM is not just software, but a strategic approach to customer relationship management that can improve the way your organization interacts with customers. It is not surprising that according to the Snov.io resource, 91% of companies with more than 10 employees already use CRM systems to optimize customer service and increase efficiency.

In this chapter, we will look at how using a business CRM can be a critical factor in scaling your company and analyze the benefits of implementing a CRM system for marketplaces, such as improved customer interactions, optimized sales, and increased levels of operational efficiency.

We'll also cover key strategies and practical tips for using these systems to grow your business and increase its profitability. Get ready to discover how implementing CRM can transform your company and help you reach new heights in the world of innovation.

What are CRM systems?

CRM for services, or customer relationship management systems, are integrated software products that specialize in storing, managing, and analyzing information about customers and their interactions with the company. They are used to automate and streamline processes such as contact management, sales management, marketing campaigns, and customer service.

The main goal of CRM systems for commodity businesses is to improve relationships with customers and increase their loyalty and satisfaction, which in turn leads to increased sales volumes and profitability. These systems allow businesses to collect information about users from various sources through Facebook automation, track their interactions with the company, analyze this data, and use it to make strategic decisions.

One of the key functions of CRM systems for online stores is the storage of a centralized customer database, in which you can store information about customer contact details, the history of their orders, interactions, and other important details. This allows employees from different departments of the company to easily access this information and effectively interact with users.

In addition, CRM helps manage sales, including tracking potential and current deals, connecting payment systems to the site, managing the sales funnel, and forecasting. They provide tools for creating and tracking marketing campaigns, as well as analyzing their effectiveness.

Also, one of the advantages of Ukrainian CRM systems such as SITNIKS, Zoho CRM, etc. is their ability to integrate with LeadForm and other business systems, such as warehouse management systems, accounting programs, and email. This allows businesses to create a fully integrated business management system, resulting in increased efficiency and streamlined workflows.

So, online shopping CRMs play an important role in the modern business world, helping businesses improve customer relationship management, improve service, and increase profits. Their use is becoming essential for companies that seek to remain competitive in the face of constant changes in the market.

Benefits of using CRM systems to scale your business

Using CRM for online trading and business scaling opens up many advantages that help companies grow and develop in the market. Below we look at some of the key benefits of this approach:

Centralized data storage

CRM systems for wholesale trade provide the ability to store all information about customers, contacts, transactions, and interaction history in one centralized database. This makes it easier for all departments of the company to access and helps reduce data scattering.

Improved customer service

CRM allows businesses to more effectively track and respond to the needs of their customers. Through data analytics, companies can provide personalized services and products, which increases their loyalty and satisfaction.

Increased employee productivity

Automating with Facebook and streamlining other routine tasks such as ticket processing, contact tracing, and appointment scheduling allows employees to spend more time on important strategic tasks and customer interactions.

Effective sales management

CRM systems help you track deals, forecast sales, and identify potential growth opportunities. This allows you to optimize the sales process and increase sales volumes.

Analysis and optimization of marketing campaigns.

CRM for business allows you to track the effectiveness of marketing campaigns, as well as identify the most promising channels of communication with customers. This helps businesses focus on strategies that are most effective for their audience.

Business scaling

By eliminating routine tasks and improving management efficiency, Ukrainian CRM systems allow companies to pay more attention to strategic growth and business scaling. This may include expanding markets, developing new products or services, and identifying new development opportunities.

Using the best CRM systems for small businesses to scale organizations allows businesses to optimize customer interactions, and improve productivity and management efficiency, which contributes to the overall growth and success of the company.

Steps to successfully scaling your business

Scaling your business with the best CRM systems is a complex process that requires careful planning and many steps. Below we will look in detail at the main steps that need to be taken into account when scaling a business using CRM:

Business needs assessment

The first step is to thoroughly examine your business needs and goals. Be sure to identify which specific areas of your business need optimization and automation with CRM. This could be sales management, marketing campaigns, customer service, etc.

Choosing a suitable CRM system

Once you've identified your needs, do your research and choose the best small business CRM that suits your wants. Consider functionality, scalability, cost, and ease of implementation.

Integration and implementation planning

Next, you should develop a detailed plan for integrating a CRM system for wholesale trade into your business. Try to define implementation steps, distribute responsibilities between employees, and determine time frames for each stage.

System setup and configuration

One thing to remember when implementing a CRM is to note the need to customize the system according to the specific needs of your business. This may include creating custom forms, setting access rights, setting up workflows, and the like.

Staff training and support

An equally important step is to ensure that your staff are trained in using CRM for medium-sized businesses. High-quality training of employees will help make the most of the system's capabilities and increase work productivity several times.

Implementation of the system into the work process

Once you have completed setting up and training your staff, you should begin implementing CRM for a product business into your workflow. Slowly and gradually migrate all the necessary data and tasks into the system and ensure its daily use.

Monitoring and analysis of results

Once the system is implemented, its effectiveness and results should be continuously monitored. Regularly analyze data, monitor performance indicators, and make the necessary adjustments to optimize processes.

Continuous improvement and development

Remember that the CRM system must be flexible and ready to change. Try to constantly look for opportunities to improve and develop the system, taking into account the needs of your business and changes in the market.

Be sure to consider that the overall success of scaling your business using a wholesale CRM system depends on a deep understanding of your organization's needs, the right system selection, and the right implementation and usage strategy.

10

How do we build the perfect team to make cooperation effective?

Building a well-functioning team is not easy. This activity can be quite a challenge. Despite this, it is worth spending some time on it and creating a group that will motivate and help each other, and have a common goal.

Identifying the team's needs and problems is extremely important. For this purpose, we can use individual interviews, control questions, or anonymous surveys. This can create a joint discussion that will help build an efficient team. So how do we build an effective and well-coordinated team that will achieve the set goals easily and without any problems? How to start building an effective team?

What is a team?

A team is a specific number of people with a common goal. Each of them is aware that to achieve it, their commitment is needed. This group also has team methods of collaboration, making it efficient and effective.

Building a team means an appropriate selection of individual employees who have similar competencies and personalities. It is also important to determine the appropriate moment to transfer the task to another employee.

What are the advantages of building a team that achieves set goals?

In a well-coordinated team, individual members are more oriented to the needs of their colleagues. There is a better flow of information between them and they are aware of their strengths and strengths. A well-coordinated, ideal team avoids conflicts, looks for the best solutions, obtains the best results from its teamwork, and is aware of its goals that can be achieved. It is also important that there is mutual trust between group members so that they can support each other at every stage of project creation.

How to build an effective team?

A manager may have quite a dilemma when selecting team members. The people he selects for the team must be able to jointly define the final vision of a given project or tolerate differences of opinion between individual people, and most importantly - they must also be able to work alone. So what should you consider when building your team?

Do you need support in building a team from scratch? HR Project offers support in the form of the HR Director by Hour service. Thanks to this, you will gain the support of a practitioner with extensive experience in creating efficient project teams.

Trust between people in the team

Team identity and trust between its members demonstrate a type of affiliation that contributes to a willingness to cooperate. If there is a lack of trust in the team, hidden action plans, unfulfilled expectations or contradictory information may appear.

Motivating

The team's motivation involves injecting energy and awareness of responsibility into it. A motivated team means not only working together at the highest level but also mutual training, new experiences, and the opportunity to solve problems together.

Communication

Communication is an extremely important factor for any group of employees. Thanks to it, feedback and tips are provided. Effective communication means more benefits not only for the team leader but also for all colleagues in the group. Thanks to it, they can get to know each other better, which will certainly facilitate cooperation in the team.

Band leader

We cannot forget about the person whose task is to manage the team. It is the group leader who responds to the team's motivation, resolves conflicts, shows them the way, and supports them.

Stress tolerance

It is extremely important in the team's work. Co-workers are aware of time pressure, time constraints, and work-life balance.

11

How to build an effective and efficient team of employees?

Every week, even the best-organized teams encounter obstacles that make it difficult for them to operate effectively within the organization. The most common problems include unproductive meetings, excess e-mails, and lack of awareness of what other colleagues are working on. These are the elements that can prevent the team from crossing subsequent items off the to-do list, create chaos in the team's activities prevent them from being performed effectively, and also introduce confusion in communication.

4 essential tools that will help a manager create an effective and efficient team

This will ultimately lead to great disorganization and discouragement and create a significant challenge in building an effective team. Therefore, the role of the leader is not only to consciously manage the team, based on support, communication, and appropriate tools but also to respond to crises that arise in the group. We present tools that are an effective way for managers and leaders to create an effective work environment and support healthy teamwork to improve overall team performance and build an effective team of employees.

It doesn't matter whether you are a manager or leader of a large or small team. Think about your most inspiring team - one that people want to join, that achieves goals, holds passionate meetings, and consistently exceeds expectations. What makes this happen and why people are engaged and effective? An appropriate management strategy that will allow you to achieve the organization's goals and at the same time meet the needs of employees. A study of hundreds of teams revealed four factors that significantly distinguish high-performing groups that create effective and efficient employee teams. Teams that perform average on all four have an 83% chance of receiving a high-performance rating, while teams in the top quartile have a 96% chance.

Here are the four factors mentioned:

1. Take care of the mental comfort of team members.

Highly performing teams need a safe space. They are created by people who are sure that the team supports each other and operates based on healthy relationships and principles of cooperation. In which there is no place for unhealthy actions, gossip, clipping of wings, or a strong attempt to dominate either one of the employees or the leader. Psychological comfort in the team is achieved by paying attention to building and maintaining trust. Team members demonstrate their commitment to each other by actively cooperating and supporting each other. It is also about creating a safe space to express who they are and are appreciated for their commitment to the results of the entire team.

2. Leverage your employees' talents

High-performing teams are diverse. Each team member brings different experiences to the team, both personal and professional. Everyone can mutually and actively engage their diverse perspectives and talents to expand the team's capabilities, test new ideas, and see more aspects and consequences of their work. Sometimes leading to heated discussions, which are also needed in the organization. However, avoiding conflicts between employees significantly reduces team commitment and, in the worst case, may lead to the loss of valuable employee resources.

3. Think big High-

performing teams focus on the big picture. They ask: "What is good for the company?" They focus on creating business value, not just achieving functional goals. By adopting a strategic enterprise perspective, they avoid making "either/or" decisions that involve false trade-offs between functional or individual interests. Instead, they seek "both/and" solutions that address tensions in competing means or priorities.

4. Work together

High-performing teams work together. They are skilled at building plans for joint action, delegating tasks, and holding each other accountable. They involve others who will be impacted by decisions while executing them quickly. They also actively engage people outside the team who have valuable perspectives or who can contribute to the quality of the team's activities.

How else can a manager improve team effectiveness?

Are you wondering where to start implementing these rules, especially if there is a conflict in the group? Remember that your team always keeps an eye on you and will require guidance and conscious action from the manager, also in the event of a crisis. Here are three solutions to start with.

1. Try the "both/and" method

Constructive conflict arises when teams think strategically together. Bring different people into the discussion. Urge the team to consider the pros and cons of different options and whether a combination rather than a single option might be a better outcome.

What does it mean? The fact that "both/and" means that the choice between two options is often "yes" and not one or the other. This appeals to the diverse perspectives of employees and doubles down on the idea of "unleashing genius." By saying yes to integrating more options, your team members will see themselves as fully engaged and encouraged to commit fully to the group's tasks.

Remember that effective team building does not necessarily require staying the same; it is worth changing your paradigm to broaden your perspective. This will allow you to understand what is happening in the team.

2. Appreciate and communicate

A relentless focus on entrepreneurship allows your team to solve problems in a broader context, not just the interests of the individual or the organization. So involve senior and junior staff in your meetings to help your team think about how to add more value to processes that impact other groups. Also, appreciate their commitment and communicate which activities bring good results and which ones are worth working on.

Communication is of great importance here. Especially since clarity often helps avoid unintentional conflicts and misunderstandings among employees. Simply by discussing the obstacles in question on an ongoing basis. There may also be opportunities to engage lower-level groups earlier and improve overall company performance.

3. Ask questions and listen carefully

Curiosity can be your superpower if you use it properly. Good leaders ask questions and seek to understand rather than tell. Just because they lead a team doesn't mean they have to dominate it. Talking and learning about the needs and talents of employees certainly works to the advantage of every manager.

Asking questions about individual stages of work and ideas will also have a positive impact on the individual commitment of individual employees. And it will help solve emerging problems. Also how they can improve their work and the work of other departments of the organization. So encourage your team members to be curious and aware of the impact of what they do on other parts of the organization.

12

How to Grow Your Business Through Marketing

Starting a new company takes a lot of time and effort, and is not an easy process. You must refine your offer, choose the best sales channels, learn more about your target market, and other things.

But no matter how good your product or service is, no one will know about it unless you advertise your company. Building your brand and generating leads for your small business requires marketing.

In this chapter, we'll look at some of the best marketing strategies to help you expand your small business's clientele and reputation.

So let's start right now.

Set your business growth goals

Please do this if you have time to sit down and do one thing. Set growth goals for your small business.

You may need more money from investors, so keep an eye out for successful startup pitch examples.

This is not easy to implement if you don't understand the rationale behind your small business's growth plans.

Do you want to sign a contract with two new large buyers? Looking for a distributor in another region? Are you thinking about opening a new location? Consider diversifying into another line of products or services.

Please give it a title and a time frame, whatever it may be.

Knowing why you do marketing can help you understand how to use it to grow your small business.

Simply articulating your goals can have a significant impact on how you find clients, how your sales team advances projects, and much more. Therefore, decide on your goals and communicate them before starting the marketing process.

When everyone in the office knows the goals, even in a tiny office of five, working toward them is much easier.

Find out about your target audience

What do your customers want? Who are they? Think about their interests, geography, gender, and age. The easier it is to create a marketing message that resonates, the better you will understand the demographics of your target customer.

Explore the short-term field of marketing

It is critical to understand the ROI as early as possible as you scale. Then you will have the momentum and cash flow to work on more ambitious projects, long-term strategies, and sustainable growth models.

Since you won't get a return on your investment as quickly as you'd like, strategies that take time to grow (like SEO) are a poor choice for achieving your primary goals.

Place some of your eggs in other baskets if you have enough resources to start with them.

Paid advertising can provide a quick return on investment if you demonstrate that people are searching on Google to purchase your solution.

Double down on what works

Pay attention to the statistics once your initiatives are up and running and you've tried a few different things. This can help you find out what is effective. Double down on proven income strategies as you grow.

Create an SEO Friendly Website

Any new company should have a website, such as Wix or Weebly so that customers can learn more about it and purchase its products or services.

You've already passed the first hurdle if you develop a website that's optimized for search engines and conversions.

Before spending money on other marketing strategies, you should focus on increasing organic website traffic.

It would be helpful if you thought about the following:

1. Create high-quality content on popular topics in your field.
2. Before creating content for your website, conduct an intensive keyword search.
3. Include primary keywords in titles, meta descriptions, and other content on your site's landing pages.
4. To make your site's SERP listings perform better and stand out from your competitors, use structured data.
5. Pay more attention to long-tail keywords and local SEO.
6. Take care of the technical elements of SEO, such as website design and page load time.
7. While there are many factors to consider when creating an SEO-optimized website, the following guidelines can help.

As I mentioned before, finding time to work is key to small business marketing.

Focus on marketing strategies you have time for

If you're like many other small firms, you're short-staffed and most team members have multiple roles. Nobody has the time to learn how to run a complex Google Ads campaign or understand how Instagram Reels works.

Use strategies that will produce the best results with the time you have, whether it's 5 hours a month or 5 hours a week.

For example, building a complex email flow is not the best use of your time if you allocate 5 hours a month to marketing activities.

This is a fantastic marketing strategy and would be very helpful to you in nurturing the leads you already have in your system, but:

You may not even complete this workflow in 5 hours and it won't give you the best value for your money.

There are plenty of tips and lead-generation marketing strategies for small and medium businesses at your disposal, including

- Event Marketing
- Paid advertising
- Conversational Marketing
- Social media marketing
- Testing and optimization of your website for lead generation
- Email marketing
- Blogs

The list is endless. They cannot be completed all at once.

Remember your small business goals. How did you want to expand your small company?

Which of these strategies will help you achieve your goal faster?

Start with the most compatible strategies with your goals and target market. There is no point in getting too spread out and exhausted. Instead, choose one or two strategies that you know will help you achieve your goals and focus your efforts until you start to see results.

Encourage satisfied customers to leave reviews

Your product or service looks like a smart investment when a satisfied consumer praises it on social media or a review site. Word of mouth plays an important role in a person's purchasing decision, even on social media.

A potential customer is more likely to come to you if they see a friend talking about your business on Facebook or if they post a photo of food from your restaurant on Instagram.

Social media recommendations make 71% of consumers more likely to make a purchase.

Encourage customers to review your product on Yelp, Google, or social media if they tell you they like it.

If you have a physical store, you can also post signs with your account handles so consumers know who to tag if they post photos of your products.

Track progress and make changes

Every marketing attempt fails sometimes. Stay alert to which marketing messages are effective and which are not, as well as the best media outlets.

The "set it and forget it" strategy does not apply to marketing. As you learn more about your target audience, media consumption habits, and purchasing preferences, constant monitoring of critical metrics and adjustments will be required.

13

Optimizing Your Business for Long-Term Success

Optimizing your business for long-term success involves focusing on customer retention, streamlining operations, investing in marketing and innovation, monitoring key performance indicators, and diversifying revenue streams. By setting clear financial goals, analyzing financial statements, and consistently reviewing long-term business goals, you can secure sustainable growth and maximize profitability.

Continuous Learning and Skill Development

In the current, variable, and uncertain business environment, an organization's survival in a competitive market is determined by its "resources". And it is no longer about the brand, portfolio of products or services, financial capital, or even real estate and movable property. It is primarily about human resources and the potential they contain, as well as opportunities for further development in various, often non-obvious and yet unknown areas. They guarantee the creation of innovations and new processes, services, and products.

However, to make this possible, employees must have the skill that is currently most desired by employers - constant learning, i.e. the predisposition and willingness to constantly learn, supplement, and expand their competencies in the process of continuous learning. The organization's key goal is to maintain its market position through continuous development, adapted to the needs and expectations of the business. To achieve this goal, however, it is necessary to know your resources in the form of knowledge about internal competencies and the ability to assign them appropriate roles, now and in the future.

This action requires improving coherence and cooperation between various functions and specializations, as well as increasing the internal mobility of employees, based on their competencies and continuous learning skills. It is easier to invest smaller resources in supplementing the knowledge and experience of those already employed than to look for new resources on the market where the fight for an employee continues for good and the price to be paid for him is getting higher and higher.

What is continuous learning?

Constant learning is the ability to constantly learn, which consists of willingness, motivation, and perseverance in acquiring knowledge and experience to improve one's competencies and allow oneself to develop in other areas in the future. It is part of personal and professional development, which is intended to prevent stagnation and help use the full potential of every professionally active person. The ongoing learning process itself can take various forms - from formal courses, development programs, or studies, to free social learning. However, it is inherently related to own initiative and taking up challenges. It may take place both within the organization or be more personal, for example as part of lifelong learning. This skill is currently considered one of the most important and characteristic of the employees of the future.

Growth mindset

The human brain develops through learning, and learning itself is an important element influencing mental well-being and increasing self-confidence and self-esteem. Lifelong learning is associated with greater employability, satisfaction, optimism, and a better ability to derive the most benefit from one's actions, and working and living on a continuous learning curve gives you an advantage in an unstable work environment. Gaining knowledge and new experiences - whether practical skills or theoretical knowledge, always pays off. Having them can not only make entries in your CV more attractive, and improve your lifestyle or the amount of earnings, but above all, it allows you to discover the hidden talents in every person. Improving your learning skills and adopting a "growth" attitude by employees pays off not only for people active in the labor market but above all for the organizations that employ them.

Why is the ability of employees to constantly learn so important for an organization?

Maintaining a competitive position in today's changing global market is associated with innovation, adaptability, and openness to constant changes. Achieving such a state by any organization depends on the skills and knowledge of employees, as well as their approach to continuous development. Unfortunately, acquiring employee resources that have the necessary competencies and, above all, those who want to constantly develop is not an easy task. Creating innovations, setting up a new process, or introducing a product or service to the market requires learning, at almost all levels, because to find their way in the new reality and take the next step, people need knowledge and skills. Therefore, if a company neglects and does not support the continuous learning process, innovations are not produced, processes remain unchanged, and achieving or creating something new is impossible.

Currently, employees, regardless of their position, must be able to set themselves challenges and cope with those put before them by their employer and the market. All this is to acquire new knowledge and skills and, as a result, create new ideas. The learning process must therefore take place in a flexible, continuous, and on-demand manner so that it can continuously contribute to the results achieved by the organization.

What can an organization do to encourage continuous learning?

It is unrealistic to expect all employees to engage in continuous learning during the working day, or even more so during their free time. However, it is a good starting point for considering how to start building an effective learning environment in the organization.

However, the most important thing in this whole process is three key elements:

1. Continuous learning starts with leaders

When employees see that their manager is fully engaged and supports learning and development initiatives, as well as constantly developing himself, it creates an atmosphere conducive to continuous learning.

Sometimes employees find it difficult to break away from their daily work tasks because they may believe that management may not approve. Showing employees that such an attitude is important and appreciated by managers becomes a role model.

2. Study plan

When continuous learning becomes part of the entire organization's operations, employees are more likely to engage in continuous learning. This means defining the business goals you want to achieve and creating an actionable plan on how to support them. Engaging in dialogue about continuous learning means that employees will not only see that the organization supports learning initiatives, but that efforts are being made to make this a reality.

The plan may include information about what resources or support individuals may need or what types of learning can be offered to ensure that each employee feels their needs in this area will be met. It is also good if each employee interested in their development receives their plan for continuous learning and competence improvement.

3. Provide resources and time for continuous learning

The main element of creating a learning environment is time and resources. They must be available to all employees at all times. This environment can take many shapes and forms, depending on the needs of the organization, department, or individual employees.

Examples include:

1. Personal development plans are established for each employee to determine what they may want to learn to effectively support their willingness and initiative,
2. Consent to allocate specific working time for employees to participate in training or learning.
3. Providing access to professional resources through subscriptions or memberships.
4. Providing access to online learning and self-paced courses.
5. Organization of mentoring or coaching programs.

Organization of workshops or team events. In the modern work environment, everyone is forced to adapt and expand their skills. Organizations must provide conditions in which not only emphasis is placed on continuous learning, but, above all, it provides the opportunity to constantly deepen knowledge and gain experience in a manner tailored to the individual needs of each employee. Training or any development program should not be viewed as a one-time event that occurs after moving to a new role or project, it should be viewed as an ongoing process that does not end as long as the employee is employed in the organization.

Creating a learning culture in your organization is an effective way to improve productivity and innovation, but also employee satisfaction and retention. The more employees know and the more they can do, the more they can contribute to the organization. Therefore, if they want to develop, they should do everything to enable them to develop continuously. It will be increasingly difficult to find good, experienced, and motivated employees who are open to constant development and change. Therefore, it is worth appreciating and investing in those you already have as soon as possible.

Change management

Change often creates resistance among people, especially in complex systems such as those involved in manufacturing. Hence the concept of change management, which turns out to be particularly important in the current, extremely turbulent economic reality.

What is change management?

The concept of change management essentially means a multi-stage process whose aim is to implement modifications and maintain them. The aim of such improvements is most often to improve the company's competitiveness and profitability, especially through modifications in the production cycle.

Stages of change management

To make this possible, change management must have appropriate stages, the most common of which are:

1. Recognizing that change is needed

For this purpose, data and observations are necessary, which can be collected thanks to appropriate technological solutions.

2. Communication within the company (and often also outside it)

As we mentioned, change often creates resistance among people who are more comfortable with the status quo. That is why it is so important to indicate how beneficial its impact will be on the processes and, of course, above all, on the people involved.

3. Monitoring the progress of the change

Every management process must involve monitoring. Otherwise, we are unable to assess whether the modification brings benefits. The method of monitoring must be planned before the change is introduced.

4. Checking the effects and making any corrections

Often, modifications are also necessary in the process. Stubbornly sticking to your assumptions, if the change is not beneficial at first glance, may result in financial losses and loss of trust among employees.

5. Sustaining the change

Systems often tend to revert to their original state if they are not kept in their new position long enough. That is why it is so important to be aware of what change management is in terms of the stages of its implementation and how much employees have a role in it.

Examples of change management in production organizations

The reality in manufacturing companies is never stable and one-dimensional. These companies are constantly faced with changes, e.g. in the costs of raw materials and their availability, as well as employee turnover. All this with the primary goal of maintaining the company's profitability and, ultimately, its development.

Hence, the change for such entities is primarily the continuous optimization of various types of processes thanks to appropriate technological solutions. However, to spot areas requiring modification, it is necessary to constantly monitor the production status. The basis for changes is specific data, the collection of which does not have to be demanding. Modern systems based on digital or analog sensors that analyze various aspects of the production process, especially its speed, can help with this. Thus, information is obtained about production efficiency and possible critical points, as well as whether everything is consistent with the assumptions.

However, if the indicators deviate from optimal, changes are necessary. They may include, for example, the implementation of a modern MES system for production management, additional training for employees, or a comprehensive reorganization of the production cycle to improve its efficiency. An example of modification is also the modernization of the machinery to a more efficient one.

As you can see, change management requires an appropriate approach to push through and maintain it. This process may be demanding, but you should not be afraid of the modifications themselves. In the current, rapidly changing economic reality, stagnation is a way to quickly fail and be overtaken by market competitors.

IV

Advanced Strategies and Tips for Wholesaling Success

14

How to attract financing for a business at different stages

To develop a business, you need funds - the entrepreneur's savings or money from external sources. We talk about attracting financing from private investors, banks, and special funds

Why investment is needed

Investment is an external financial flow that supports a business at the start, at the development stage, and until the moment when it begins to generate stable profits. Investor money can be used to buy equipment, rent premises or hire staff.

Businesses often require financial support from outside even during periods of stable operation. However, many investors refuse to invest in a project until it has reached its potential.

According to the US Federal Bureau of Labor Statistics and the research company Startup Genome, up to 75% of newly created organizations do not survive to the stage of bringing the idea to life. In 30–40% of cases, the funds invested in them are completely lost.

Meanwhile, attracting financing from external sources helps support a business during its formation and development.

Stages of company development

Regardless of the type of activity, companies go through:

The initial stage: During which the products are developed and brought to market; at this stage, according to statistics from researchers from Startup Genome, up to 90% of startups close with losses for investors;

Expansion stage: This occurs after the development and implementation of the business model; it is characterized by sales growth and constant cash flow;

Growth stage: When the company receives a stable income and strengthens its position in the market.

At every stage, it is impossible to do without financing. At the start, it helps the company create the first product samples or test the chosen business model. At the expansion stage - promote the product or enter foreign markets. Investments in a mature enterprise ensure the modernization of production, the absorption of competitors, or the search and development of new directions.

Types of Business Finance

There are two ways to raise funds:

Equity investment

It involves transferring part of the business to a financial partner. He becomes a co-owner of the enterprise, influences organizational or work processes, and receives a share of the profits.

Debt financing

We are talking about obtaining a loan that is repaid within a specified time with the payment of interest. The business owner retains control of the enterprise. However, banks often refuse loans to companies that are at an early stage due to high risks. In the next two stages, this type of financing can be actively used.

How to choose the type of financing

When attracting financing, you need to decide whether it will be a loan with interest or equity participation from the investor. To do this, weigh the pros and cons of each option.

An equity partnership is less profitable for the owner of the company since he will have to constantly give part of the profit to the investor. At the same time, the participation of third-party people or companies in the business allows you to optimize work processes and establish connections with other market participants.

If an entrepreneur plans to attract borrowed capital, he will have to comply with the conditions of a lender, for example, a bank. At the same time, it is important to assess the potential and profitability of the business taking into account the value of assets and the size of accounts receivable.

Principles of searching for investors

Businesses at different stages of development may have different sources of financing. Thus, at the initial stage, they usually use their capital, funds from acquaintances or friends, or the help of private investors.

At the stages of expansion and growth, venture funds, direct or strategic investments, and banks are attracted. Mature companies are helped by banks or private equity funds.

Sources of funding for startups

Newly created companies can count on the following sources of funds:

Friends or acquaintances

It is easier and faster to raise this money. But this method has a drawback: if the enterprise fails and difficulties arise with repaying debts, relationships with loved ones may deteriorate.

Private investors who finance companies in the early stages of development are business angels. Some people invest money in an enterprise and receive a part of it in return. Then they resell it for profit. Others choose the dividend model and receive a fixed share of the growing income. Project development can be accelerated by attracting a partner with experience or connections.

Business incubators

They offer startup founders training courses or client search services. They help build a business model for a future enterprise. True, the owner of the company has to look for sources of financing himself.

Corporate growth accelerators

Interested in finding and developing startups to implement ideas within the corporation. After the launch of the pilot project, it becomes possible to start working with a large customer.

Grants from government and commercial foundations

They are selected based on the results of competitions. You can spend money on pre-agreed purposes; this must be confirmed by reports. To participate in the competition you need to submit an application and prepare a package of documents.

Investment clubs

They bring together private investors who search for startups and present them at community meetings. You can contact the club through an application on the website or social networks.

Crowdfunding

Allows you to raise funds from several private investors through special platforms. The business can use the money received at its discretion.

Venture funds

They distribute investor funds and are focused on the international market. To apply for funding, you need to send a project presentation with explanations to the fund's email.

Sources of financing at the stages of business expansion and growth

Enterprises often go through the initial stage at the expense of the owner or founders' funds. However, further funding is required. Money is needed to scale the project or increase the volume of production of goods in demand on the market.

As a rule, legal entities finance mature companies. They receive interest on loans or profits from equity interests in the business.

A business that is already operating can use the following external sources of funds:

Investment funds

They invest in profitable projects. They receive a share in the business, which they then sell to strategic partners at an increased rate. The websites of these funds usually have a list of services, terms of cooperation, and a feedback form.

Strategic investment funds

They buy companies to make a profit. Such investors independently search for projects that interest them.

Banks that provide financing to individuals and companies. They have a conservative approach and work with organizations that can repay the loan with interest payments. To get a loan on favorable terms, you can first open a current account at your chosen bank or connect a salary project. This will increase the chances of success but does not guarantee it.

Lack of a clear development plan

If an entrepreneur does not have a clear business model, it is too early to raise financing. Investors will not agree to invest in a project with vague prospects, since their goal is to protect free capital from inflation and make a profit.

An attempt to revive a company that has lost its market or large customers

It is unlikely that in such a situation it is worth thinking about external financing as a means of salvation. Often such a business has debt obligations, the enterprise operates on outdated equipment or produces products that cannot be sold.

Business valuation methods

The following methods allow you to assess the profitability and prospects of a project:

Fixed cost method

It is used to attract resources in the early stages of business development when its future is most uncertain. Companies involved in financing such projects invest a fixed amount in exchange for an agreed share in the business.

Venture capital method

It is based on an assessment of the current state of affairs and the theoretical profitability that the investor wants to receive. For example, a company plans to reach a market value of x rubles in five years, and an investor expects a 20-fold profit. The starting price of the business is taken as x/20, the ratio of the amount of attracted capital to the initial cost of the project determines the investor's share.

Discounted cash flow method

Based on a detailed financial development forecast with a horizon of at least three years. The planning period corresponds to the payback period and depends on the characteristics of the business. For example, the forecast for a small store or training center is made for three years; for projects that require large investments, the model is calculated with a perspective of five to seven years.

15

Management of Legal Risks and Legal Issues

Managing legal risks and legal issues becomes a priority for key stakeholders, including stakeholders such as the board of directors and regulators. In many companies, the lack of a clear legal risk analysis can lead to difficulties that leave the legal department forced to respond on an ad hoc basis. However, such problems can be avoided by creating a system and developing a proactive risk management strategy.

Because conventional approaches and industry standards for proactive risk management are slow to evolve, organizations do not have appropriate strategies. As a result, many managers cannot be fully confident that they are adequately managing risks in the following areas:

1. Litigation
2. Changes in legislation
3. Contract management
4. Data Confidentiality

Customized solutions and actionable analytics

Working closely with your legal department, we ensure the following:

1. Assessing the current state of risk management processes.
2. Non-conformity analysis.
3. We are developing a road map to eliminate existing inconsistencies, including providing recommendations on selecting IT solutions.

A proven four-step approach

When developing a system that an organization can use to manage activities based on risk limits, our experts use a clear four-step process:

Analysis. Analysis of the risk structure to identify legal risks that can significantly affect the organization's strategy and achievement of its business goals.

Grade. Creation and implementation of a process for assessing the degree of impact of risks (the assessment is carried out based on an approved set of risk factors, which includes regulatory, customer, financial, reputational, and other risks).

Control. Implementation of a control system to keep residual legal risks within risk appetite.

Monitoring and reporting. Development of a methodology for assessing the effectiveness of the control system. Preparation of reports with the results of the analysis of residual risks in terms of their impact on the effectiveness of the legal department and the functioning of control mechanisms (reports are prepared for management responsible for the relevant area of corporate governance).

16

Negotiation strategies

Each of the negotiating parties pursues specific goals, which (provided that the preparation is carried out effectively) are clear to all parties to the negotiations. But, be that as it may, each of the participants, whether he understands it or not, also pursues another goal, which is to manage the communication process. This is why negotiation strategies are used.

It is important to understand that if the goals of the negotiators do not completely coincide, which, by the way, happens in most cases, it is the one who manages the negotiation process who wins. Management here means choosing the most active position, asserting one's point of view, ensuring one's own decisions are made, insisting on certain proposals, etc.

But often the difficulty lies in the fact that, firstly, not everyone knows and understands how the negotiation process is managed, and, secondly, each of the participants can take initiative aimed at managing negotiations, which in turn can lead to complicating the situation. It is for this reason that every person should have an understanding of the ethics of the negotiation process.

Global Negotiation Conditions

Global conditions for conducting negotiations can also be characterized as a global strategy - a strategy that should be fundamental and in-depth. This is what you should rely on when building any other strategy. It is the foundation of all further actions.

The global conditions for negotiations are represented by three basic components:

1. You must clearly understand what you want to achieve in the negotiation process
2. You must be flexible in your behavior
3. You must use feedback (constantly evaluate whether your actions are moving you towards achieving your intended outcome)

Considering that we have already said enough about goal setting in the first lesson, we will dwell in more detail on the last two points - flexibility in behavior and the use of feedback.

Behavioral flexibility is a global condition for the reason that it should always manifest itself in everything, but first of all, it concerns, of course, the use of such means of communication as gestures, facial expressions, voice, manner of speaking, lexical (vocabulary), etc. .d. All this, figuratively speaking, is your means of transportation from point A (the beginning of negotiations with all its inherent features) to point B (achieving the goal). Thus, the more universal your vehicle is, the more chances you will have to achieve the desired result. Also take into account the fact that negotiations are always controlled by the person with the greatest flexibility, and behavioral rigidity and narrow-mindedness only create obstacles.

Having a clear vision of the desired outcome and flexibility are two sides of the same coin: you must always understand what you are trying to achieve and remain committed to your goal, but at the same time you must remain flexible - use different methods to achieve the goal.

As for the use of feedback, in practical terms it can be displayed like this: imagine that the negotiation process is a chess game. Seeing a chessboard with pieces located on it in front of you, you assess the state of affairs, calculate options for the development of the situation, make a move, thereby changing the playing position, and then wait for your opponent to make a move, also changing the playing position. After this, the cycle repeats, and this happens over and over again. The situation is the same with negotiations: you make a statement - you make a move, followed by a statement - your opponent's move. Next, you evaluate the situation and determine whether your statement was successful or not, and then, based on the conclusions already drawn, you build a further communication process.

It is very important to understand the dynamics of the negotiation process: initially, you try to adapt to your opponent to achieve mutual understanding. This stage is different in that you rely in your speech on what everyone already knows, citing as examples some platitudes and axioms, because your goal is to ensure that your opponent agrees with what you say. You can receive consent either in direct verbal form or in indirect form, which will be expressed in approving glances, nods, etc. But here, too, one should not lose vigilance - one should not be overly banal so as not to offend the feelings of the opponent, and also delay this stage of achieving initial agreement. If you see that the reaction to your words and comments is positive, that will already be enough.

Once the initial agreement has been reached and the general rules and principles of negotiation have been established, you can expect to have the negotiation process in your hands. Only after making sure of this can you begin to offer some options for solving the problem and ideas that can help you achieve your goal. And feedback, of course, is important here too. If you see that your opponent accepts what you are saying with approval, continue your speech, but if you begin to notice that there is no longer agreement (the interlocutors' facial expressions have changed, they have begun to look around, etc.), you should immediately return to adjustment, i.e. summarize and repeat once again what your interlocutors agreed with when you first started your speech. After this, you can begin to formulate rejected ideas in some other way, using that same behavioral flexibility.

The use of feedback can also be expressed in the fact that during the negotiations you will from time to time check the extent of your progress towards the goal by asking questions about what you have not yet discussed, as well as wondering if it is time to take stock. By the way, the latter may be perceived as a hidden command to end the negotiations. And here, once again, you must use feedback: try in any possible way to determine (notice, hear, feel) the opponent's reaction to your statements, and in no case forget about flexibility - experiment, be creative, try new behavioral techniques.

Features of negotiations involving more than two opponents

By and large, the very essence of negotiations with the participation of more than two opponents does not undergo any changes, however, such negotiations are still considered more complex, because have several specific features:

Preparation and planning of negotiations are more expensive in terms of time, collection of information, and resources involved, because the information is collected not about one participant, but about several.

Defining and setting goals is complicated by the fact that it is necessary to come to an agreement that will suit several participants at once, and therefore must satisfy a much larger number of conditions.

The choice of a negotiation strategy becomes significantly more difficult because there is a risk of falling under massive pressure, choosing an ineffective line of behavior, finding yourself in unfavorable conditions, etc.

During the negotiation process, attention should be paid not to one opposite party, but to each of them, which requires quite specific skills from each participant: it is necessary to be able to determine the reactions of several people (or groups of people), speeches must be built taking into account the personal (or group) characteristics of each of them. participants, it is required to have the ability to fend off arguments expressed by several sides, etc.

More generally speaking, the main difference between negotiations with more than two participants and negotiations with two participants lies mostly in psychological preparation and goal setting, because These two stages cause the greatest difficulties here. For this reason, third-party specialists are much more often involved in preparing for negotiations with the participation of more than two parties.

The optimal number of participants for negotiations is considered to be no more than six parties - this is the maximum number of opponents with which it is possible to develop a productive process of interaction and achieve common goals. If the number of participants in the negotiations exceeds this figure, such an event can bring any benefit only if it is informational, for example, it is devoted to getting to know points of view, receiving and exchanging information, etc. So keep this data in mind - in certain situations, it can help in making some decisions, including deciding whether or not to participate in negotiations at all.

Negotiation Strategies

The term "strategy" dates back to Ancient Greece, where it was interpreted as "the art of the commander." Currently, the meaning of this concept is used in a much broader sense, although its essence can be expressed in a simple and concise form: strategy is the basic model of action.

When we talk about strategy about the negotiation process, we mean those actions that we will take to achieve our intended result. The strategy you choose directly determines whether you achieve your goal or not. It is also interesting that in some situations the negotiation strategy can be aimed at achieving a goal at any cost, in others - at maintaining relations between opponents, in others - at adapting to the conditions of a stronger opponent, etc.

Of all the classifications of negotiation strategies, the most common and most popular is the "WIN-WIN" classification, developed by specialists at the Harvard Negotiation Project - Bruce Patton, William Ury, and Roger Fisher, and later presented by them in the work "The Path to Agreement, or Negotiations without Defeat." By the way, the "WIN-WIN" strategy is very similar to the Thomas-Kilman grid, according to which there are five styles of behavior in conflict situations: Cooperation, Competition, Compromise, Adaptation, and Evasion.

Based on the basic premises of this classification, four basic negotiation strategies are distinguished:

1. Strategy "WIN-WIN" (COLLABORATION)
2. "WIN-LOSE" strategy (COMPETITION)
3. LOSE-WIN Strategy
4. "LOSE-LOSE" strategy

A particular strategy should be determined based on two parameters: the meaning of the relationship and the meaning of the result.

Let's take a closer look at each strategy.

Strategy "WIN-WIN" (COLLABORATION)

The WIN-WIN strategy is based on cooperation. It is aimed at ensuring that all participants in the negotiations are winners at the end of the negotiations. The main prerequisite here is that opponents understand, respect, and take into account each other's interests. It is worth noting that this strategy is considered the most effective in any negotiations, and every effort should be made to find common ground with the opponent.

EXAMPLE: Vasily and Vladislav worked in the same company. Each of them strived for career growth, as a result of which both competed with each other. Vasily, like Vladislav, at every opportunity, tried to stand out and distinguish himself in some way to become better than others and, accordingly, get a more prestigious position in the company. The rivals came up with promising projects and successfully implemented them. The head of the company was quite happy with this state of affairs because the company's position in the market was getting better and better. But one day a new manager started working at the company, who had no idea that Vasily and Vladislav had staged a "race" between themselves. This leader gave them the task of completing a common project, and, as one would expect, things fell into place. The rivals wanted to prove to each other that each of them was better, and as a result the project never progressed. The rating of colleagues in the eyes of the newly arrived manager began to fall rapidly, and he ambiguously hinted to them that they might soon be fired. Vasily and Vladislav had no choice but to start working together to complete the assigned project. Colleagues began to look for ways to achieve a common result, and not about "outpacing" each other. As a result, they concluded that they were quite comfortable working together and channeling their knowledge and skills into a common direction. In the end, the desired result was achieved, and Vasily and Vladislav themselves were promoted to leadership positions, which is what they initially strived for.

"WIN-LOSE" Strategy (COMPETITION)

The "WIN-LOSE" strategy takes rivalry as its basis. It is aimed at achieving victory by the opponent who has chosen it through any effort, and the second opponent is perceived by the first as an adversary and often even an enemy. This strategy is used mainly in cases where it is not the relationship that is important, but the result. A participant operating according to such a strategy can use all possible methods to achieve his goals, including deception, methods of delusion, manipulation, etc. If we don't go to such extremes, we can say that the presented strategy is very effective in sales, when the seller needs to increase his check at all costs by selling an expensive product or several products at once. A competitive strategy is often effective only for achieving short-term goals.

EXAMPLE: A salesperson at an electronics supermarket is tasked with fulfilling a certain plan for the month, but by the end of the month he realizes that he is still far from fulfilling the plan, which means his job may be in jeopardy. As a result, the seller decides to fulfill the plan by any means. Considering that the seller is not particularly concerned about future relationships with clients, he can begin to offer buyers the most expensive goods or a huge number of related products, try to convince buyers who do not want to make a purchase, insist on their own, etc. If the seller is kind enough and manages to build his communication with clients in such a way that they simply cannot refuse, he, of course, will be able to fulfill the plan, but the likelihood that these buyers will return to this seller in the future is extremely small.

LOSE-WIN Strategy

The "LOSE-WIN" strategy is based on adaptation. In the process of negotiations, the opportunistic strategy leads to the conscious defeat of the participant who chose it and the victory of his opponent. This strategy is most effective in situations where the relationship between opponents is of particular value, and the result in a particular situation can be relegated to the background.

EXAMPLE: A manager of a small company wants to sign a contract with a large company so that his company becomes its partner. Initially, he relies on certain conditions, draws up an agreement, and hopes for a certain result. But during the negotiations, a representative of a large company says that the contract can be signed, but only on the terms of his company, which are significantly worse than those that the manager of a small company was counting on. Even though the terms of the contract do not satisfy the manager, he still signs it, because even these unfavorable conditions open up good prospects for his company.

"LOSE-LOSE" strategy

The "LOSE-LOSE" strategy is based on evasion. In the vast majority of cases, the presented strategy is used in negotiations by parties with weak positions. But there are also situations in which one of the parties resorts to deliberately provoking mutual loss in negotiations (as a rule, these are situations when one of the opponents intends to achieve his own goals through mutual loss). In addition, there is a third option for using the evasion strategy - when rivals, regardless of what the results of the negotiations are, do not want to give in to each other, in other words, they act on the principle of "neither themselves nor people."

EXAMPLE: A person who is not particularly well versed in Internet technologies visits the resource of a professional website creation studio to order a website for his online store. The developers listen to the requirements of this customer, select the most suitable option for him, and announce the price. The customer is satisfied, the deal is concluded, and an advance payment is sent. But, a little later, the customer begins to wander the Internet and accidentally discovers that a website for an online store can be created in a couple of hours, and completely free. As a result, the customer panics, believing that he was cheated out of money, deceived, and "everything is bad." The customer, who sent an advance payment to the developers, decides to return his money.

He calls the company whose specialists create a website for him and presents his claims. The developers, unable to resist the pressure of the customer, return the money to him, finding themselves the first losers in this situation. Next, the customer, who has "saved" money, can decide to either turn to a cheaper developer (a friend, for example) or even "make a website" himself. The result of this is that now for many months this customer will understand the intricacies of website creation, or will receive a "pig in a poke" from a home-grown enthusiastic specialist. Hence it turns out that the customer becomes the second loser. In the future, the customer, of course, will come to his senses and understand why the website creation studio takes money, but it will be too late.

So, we have looked at the main negotiation strategies. Which strategy to choose for each specific situation will depend on its characteristics and context. You should be guided, first of all, by the information you receive at the stage of preparation for negotiations, as well as the significance of the relationship and the result for you. If your priority is to achieve a goal, you can choose the Competitive strategy, but keep in mind that your opponent may be quite well prepared to negotiate, and even if he initially chose the Cooperation strategy, seeing how you begin to compete with him, he may begin to compete in response, putting you at risk of spontaneously adopting Accommodation or Avoidance strategies, which will have a very negative impact on your status as a negotiator.

If the most important thing for you is to preserve the relationship, and you are ready to sacrifice your aspirations, the Accommodation strategy is quite suitable for you. But here, too, not everything is so simple, because your opponent, seeing that you are "giving in", and also not attaching much importance to the relationship with you, may well begin to actively put pressure on you, as a result of which you will find yourself in a much worse position than you originally expected.

There can be a lot of options for the development of events, for which reason it is recommended to prepare for negotiations and plan them with all seriousness and care. Here it would not be superfluous to recall the flexibility and use of feedback we mentioned earlier. Feedback will always be able to show you what negotiating strategy your opponent has decided to follow, and flexibility will allow you, in an emergency, to both change individual elements of your line of behavior or change one strategy to another.

And, finally, let us remind you that the Cooperation strategy is always and everywhere considered the most productive, because only it allows the negotiating parties to achieve their goals without significant losses (and sometimes without them at all) and, at the same time, maintain and strengthen the relationship between them, which can serve as the key to effective cooperation in the future.

17

Developing Strategic Thinking

Strategic thinking is a mental process used by a person in the context of achieving success in a game or other endeavors. The result of this activity is thoughts about how to behave in the present to get something in the future.

A person who thinks strategically often asks himself the questions "What?", "Why?" And How?". He thinks in terms of months, years, and decades, and plans his life for this period, but is capable of change. The strategist knows where and why he is going. He may make mistakes, but he can notice and correct them.

How does strategy differ from tactics?

Before we figure out how to develop strategic thinking, let's try to find the answer to a very common question. This is probably what everyone asks themselves when they first encounter these concepts. If you don't pay enough attention to the topic, you can get confused and have a vague understanding of these concepts.

Let us say right away that strategy and tactics do not diverge from each other, they are on the same plane.

1. A strategy defines your long-term goals and how you plan to achieve them.
2. Tactics are much more specific and often focus on smaller steps and shorter time frames along the way. These include best practices, specific plans, resources, and so on. They are also called "initiatives".

Here are three more important points:

1. Strategy is constant and long-term, while tactics can change depending on strategic objectives.
2. Strategy and tactics work together as a means to an end. If your strategy is to climb a mountain, one of the key components of the strategy may be deciding which side of the mountain you should start climbing it on. Your tactics are what equipment you will buy, what you will take with you, your complete trip plan, etc.
3. Strategy and tactics must always be consistent with each other. You may like a particular project (i.e. tactic), but only pursue it if it fits with your long-term strategy. In short, tactics can be changed frequently (if they do not meet the requirements of the strategy), while changing the strategy will take a lot of effort and time.

Remember that the strategy must be consistent, it is like a huge ship. Whereas tactics can be changed to correctly follow the strategy.

Principles of Strategic Thinking

Observe and look for trends

Often we don't see the big picture. This happens because there is too much work to do, which leads to stress and depression. We miss key information that could help us focus, prioritize, and be proactive in problem-solving.

To think strategically, you need to make a conscious attempt every day to look at the big picture and notice trends. The world is constantly changing and often the direction is visible. This is what we should try to see.

Ask tough questions

To notice trends and truly understand the world around you, you need to ask difficult and sometimes uncomfortable questions. Questions are the language of strategy. Only a fool can think of answers.

Look for answers by asking yourself: "Where do I see myself in a year?", "What kind of person do I want to be in three years?", "What will my company be like in five years?"

Here are more questions to ask yourself right now:

1. What are my weaknesses?
2. Do I need to deal with them or can I change them?
3. What habits are holding me back?
4. What activities take up my valuable time?

Behave like a strategist

People who can think strategically can speak this language. They prioritize and sequence their thoughts. They challenge the status quo and change their assumptions.

If this all seems daunting, here are ways to sharpen your skills:

1. Add structure to your written and oral communication. Group and logically arrange your main points and keep them as brief as possible.
2. Direct your thoughts so that you talk about both the details and the big picture. When speaking in public, the same rule applies: direct the audience's attention, moving from the general to the specific.

Take time to reflect and resolve conflicts

Whatever you do, always take time to calm down and think. It's hard to change your life if you don't think about possibilities and solutions.

The main thing to understand is this: thinking is also work and the most valuable one at that. We are used to thinking that a person works when he moves a lot and creates new things. But this is not always the case.

What happens in the head affects the quality of life to a greater extent. This helps you calm down because you are bringing out the fears and doubts that show up all the time but aren't thought through carefully. Work on your internal conflicts and you will become a much more effective thinker.

Skills that help develop strategic thinking

Strategic thinking involves developing a whole set of critical skills:

Ability to use different types of thinking

Cognitive flexibility is when you can quickly switch from logical, sequential thinking to lateral, creative thinking. When developing a strategy, the second is no less important than the first.

Ability to make predictions

Predictions are the ability to imagine the future based on accumulated knowledge and intuition. Not attempts to guess or something mystical, but the ability to see connections and understand development.

Work with goals

Such people can clearly define their goals and develop a strategic plan of action for each task, broken down into sub-tasks, as well as a list of required resources and a specific timeline.

Have a flexible mindset

This means:

1. Change the plan as you go.
2. Include so-called guidelines in the plan that help track progress and notice mistakes.

A strategist has an innate ability to take initiative and anticipate change, rather than react to it only after it occurs.

Be receptive

This means reading the clues that the world around you and other people give you, as well as using your intuition correctly. Great strategic thinkers will listen, hear, and understand what is said, read, and observe what is happening.

Continuously learn

It's not enough to just create an action plan for several years ahead and start following it. You need to be in a constant state of learning. Take advantage of every opportunity to acquire new knowledge.

Take time for yourself

This means not thinking only about work and your strategy. Sometimes it's useful to take a break, completely change your occupation, and take up new hobbies.

Develop an open mind

Sometimes it's so nice to wishful thinking. But strategists don't do that: they abandon their point of view if it contradicts new facts. They know how to calm their ego, for which they receive a reward in the form of achieving a goal.

How to develop strategic thinking

Meditate

This advice was already present in the text. But it is so important that we will put it in a separate paragraph.

Strategists create connections between ideas, plans, and people that others don't see. But how can you create these connections if you never allow your mind to see them?

In other words, the clue to how to think strategically is the first word in the phrase itself: "think." And that means committing to slow down and let your mind wander.

A simple way to do this is to schedule time to reflect. The best tools: paper and pen. Time of day: morning or evening.

Expand your horizons

It is impossible to become a strategist if you are not interested in the world and the events taking place in it. But this is not enough: you need to understand human psychology, study the functioning of the brain, read scientific books, and much more.

Strategic thinking and curiosity go hand in hand. After all, the more ideas and experiences we have, the more material there is to make connections.

You can gain experience not only from books: go on a short trip, meet new people, study nature. Also, attend seminars and conferences on a variety of topics. Update yourself constantly.